KB004945

How To Sound Like A Native Korean Speaker

원어민도 깜짝 놀라는 내 한국어 발음

How To Sound Like A Native Korean Speaker

원어민도 깜짝 놀라는 내 한국어 발음

1판 1쇄 · 1st edition published	2021. 11. 22
1판 4쇄 · 4th edition published	2023. 10. 2

지은이 · Written by	TalkToMeInKorean
책임편집 · Edited by	선경화 Kyunghwa Sun, 석다혜 Dahye Seok, 김은희 Eunhee Kim
디자인 · Designed by	선윤아 Yoona Sun, 박은경 Eunkeong Park, 한보람 Boram Han, 이은정 Eunjeong Lee
일러스트레이션 · Illustrations by	박효원 Hyo-won Park
녹음 · Voice Recordings by	선현우 Hyunwoo Sun, 김예지 Yeji Kim, 유승완 Seung-wan Yu
오디오/비디오 편집 · Video Editing by	진석진 Seokjin Jin, 김석준 Sukjun Kim
펴낸곳 · Published by	롱테일북스 Longtail Books
펴낸이 · Publisher	이수영 Su Young Lee
편집 · Copy-edited by	김보경 Florence Kim
주소 · Address	04033 서울특별시 마포구 양화로 113, 3층(서교동, 순흥빌딩)
	3rd Floor, 113 Yanghwa-ro, Mapo-gu, Seoul, KOREA
이메일 · E-mail	TTMIK@longtailbooks.co.kr
ISBN	979-11-91343-19-9 13710

*이 교재의 내용을 사전 허가 없이 전재하거나 복제할 경우 법적인 제재를 받게 됨을 알려 드립니다.

*잘못된 책은 구입하신 서점이나 본사에서 교환해 드립니다.

*정가는 표지에 표시되어 있습니다.

Copyright © 2021 TalkToMeInKorean

*All rights reserved. Partial or in full copies of this book are strictly prohibited unless consent or permission is given by the publisher.

*Defective copies of this book may be exchanged at participating bookstores or directly from the publisher.

*The standard price of this book is printed on the back cover above the UPC barcode.

TTMIK - TALK TO ME IN KOREAN

How To Sound Like A Native Korean Speaker

원어민도 깜짝 놀라는 내 한국어 발음

TABLE OF CONTENTS

HOW TO USE THIS BOOK ——————————————————— 8

PREFACE —————————————————————————— 12

CHAPTER 1. ——————————————————————— 13
**The Pronunciation That Korean Learners Struggle with the Most:
Consonants**

Lesson 1-1. **Can You Tell the Difference Between ㄱ, ㅋ, and ㄲ?** 14

Lesson 1-2. **Are You Playing with a Ball or a Bean?** 18

Quiz Time 19

Lesson 2-1. **Can You Tell the Difference Between ㄷ, ㅌ, and ㄸ?** 23

Lesson 2-2. **Are You Saying That You Dusted Yourself Off or That
You Shivered?** 27

Quiz Time 28

Lesson 3-1. **Can You Tell the Difference Between ㅂ, ㅍ, and ㅃ?** 32

Lesson 3-2. **Do You Feel Pain in Your Foot or in Your Arm?** 36

Quiz Time 37

Lesson 4-1. **Can You Tell the Difference Between ㅅ and ㅆ?** 41

Lesson 4-2. **Do You Want Me to Buy It or Wrap It?** 44

Quiz Time 45

Lesson 5-1. **Can You Tell the Difference Between ㅈ, ㅊ, and ㅉ?** 49

Lesson 5-2. **Are You Asking for My Car or My Ruler?** 52

Quiz Time 53

CHAPTER 2. ──────────────────────── 58
The Pronunciation That Korean Learners Struggle with the Most: Vowels

Lesson 1-1. **Can You Pronounce 오 and 어 Differently?** 59

Lesson 1-2. **A Cup of Nosebleed in the Morning?** 62

Quiz Time 63

Lesson 2-1. **Can You Pronounce 요 and 여 Differently?** 66

Lesson 2-2. **Is It Yoga Time or Free Time?** 70

Quiz Time 71

Lesson 3-1. **Can You Pronounce 으 and 어 Differently?** 74

Lesson 3-2. **Did You Get It Wrong or Were You Robbed?** 77

Quiz Time 78

Lesson 4-1. **Can You Pronounce 우 and 으 Differently?** 82

Lesson 4-2. **Are You Saying That You Are Lucky or That You Like Silver?** 85

Quiz Time 86

CHAPTER 3. ──────────────────────── 91
How on Earth Should I Pronounce 의?

CHAPTER 4. ──────────────────────── 100
Transformers

Lesson 1-1. **Doubles in Disguise** 101

Lesson 1-2. **Decepti-consonants** 105

Lesson 1-3. **Space Bridge** 110

Lesson 1-4. **More Than Meets the Eye** 114

Lesson 2-1. **Throw Away the Rules!** 119

Lesson 2-2. **Just Memorize It!**   126

Lesson 3. **Follow My Lead!**   131

Lesson 4. **When in Rome...**   141

Lesson 5. **ㄴ, Watch Out for ㄹ.**   150

Lesson 6. **The Quiet Strength of ㅎ**   155

Lesson 7-1. **Sticky Consonants**   163

Lesson 7-2. **Morphing Consonants**   165

CHAPTER 5. ———————————————————————————————— 170
읽 Wherefore Art Thou Pronounced 익?

CHAPTER 6. ———————————————————————————————— 182
What?! I Did Not Know It Would Sound Like This!

Lesson 1. **Why Isn't 겉옷 Pronounced [거톤]?**   183

Lesson 2. **Why Isn't 꽃잎 Pronounced [꼬칩]?**   189

CHAPTER 7. ———————————————————————————————— 201
Why Don't I Sound Right?

Lesson 1. **What Is the Difference Between G and ㄱ?**   202

Lesson 2. **What Are the Differences Between N and ㄴ, and D
           and ㄷ?**   208

Lesson 3. **What Are the Differences Between M and ㅁ, and B
           and ㅂ?**   220

Lesson 4. **What Are the Differences Between L, R, and ㄹ?**   231

Lesson 5. **ㅅ the Chameleon**   237

Lesson 6. **What Is the Difference Between J and ㅈ?**   243

CHAPTER 8. ———————————————————————— 252

Not Quite English

Lesson 1.   **Sit on the Bench, Not on My Benz.**   253

Lesson 2.   **Why English Is Pronounced Differently In Korean**   259

Lesson 3.   **Native Korean Speakers vs. The Dictionary**   263

CHAPTER 9. ———————————————————————— 269

That Is Not My Name.

CHAPTER 10. ——————————————————————— 279

Do Not Get Lost on Your Way to Costco.

CHAPTER 11. ——————————————————————— 289

Correct Order, Wrong Food

Lesson 1.   **Sundae Blues**   290

Lesson 2   **Why Are Olives So Hard to Find?**   294

CHAPTER 12. ——————————————————————— 299

There Is No Gang in Gangnam.

CHAPTER 13. ——————————————————————— 308

To Avoid Stress, Correct Your Stress

Lesson 1.   **Highs and Lows**   309

Lesson 2.   **What Did You Eat? vs. Did You Eat Something?**   319

CHAPTER 14. ——————————————————————— 329

The Dictionary Is Wrong?!

BONUS: The Short-Long Debate ———————————— 341

GLOSSARY ————————————————————————— 345

HOW TO USE THIS BOOK

Make sure to read this before you study with this book!

1. Download Our Audio App

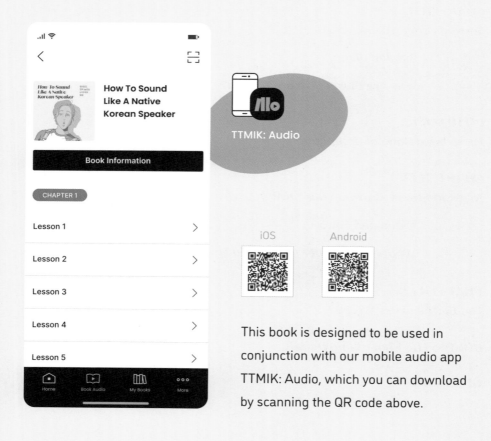

TTMIK: Audio

iOS

Android

This book is designed to be used in conjunction with our mobile audio app TTMIK: Audio, which you can download by scanning the QR code above.

TTMIK: Audio has both audio files and animated videos for this book to help you better understand tongue position and mouth shape when pronouncing a specific letter.

2. Indication of Long Vowels (ː)

문의 ⇨ [무ː늬] ⇨ [무ː니]

While studying with this book, you will see a lot of square brackets that contain phonetic transcriptions of words and sounds. In the brackets you will also occasionally see the mark ː throughout the book. This mark indicates a prolonged sound, or a long vowel in other words. If you would like to learn more about prolonged sounds, check out The Short-Long Debate on page 342.

Use this quick guide to help you navigate and decide what to study first.

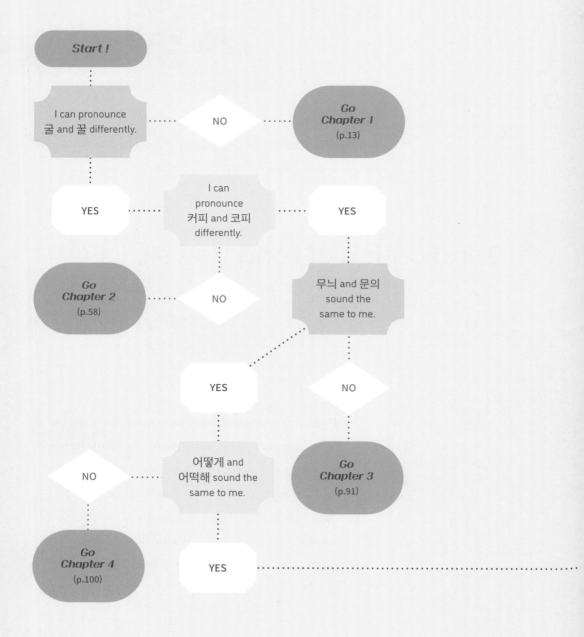

Start !

I can pronounce 굴 and 꿀 differently.

NO

Go Chapter 1 (p.13)

YES

I can pronounce 커피 and 코피 differently.

YES

Go Chapter 2 (p.58)

NO

무늬 and 문의 sound the same to me.

YES

NO

NO

어떻게 and 어떡해 sound the same to me.

Go Chapter 3 (p.91)

Go Chapter 4 (p.100)

YES

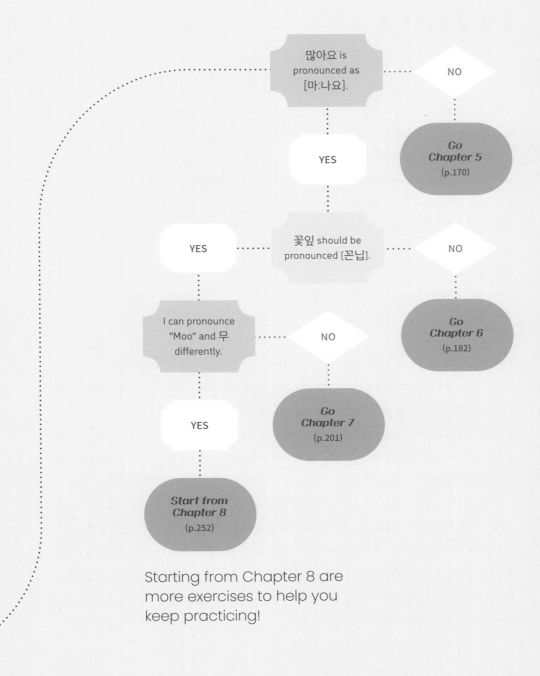

많아요 is pronounced as [마:나요].

NO

YES

Go Chapter 5 (p.170)

YES

꽃잎 should be pronounced [꼰닙].

NO

Go Chapter 6 (p.182)

I can pronounce "Moo" and 무 differently.

NO

YES

Go Chapter 7 (p.201)

Start from Chapter 8 (p.252)

Starting from Chapter 8 are more exercises to help you keep practicing!

PREFACE

Learning new sounds and practicing your pronunciation are some of the first things you do when you learn a new language. However, even after you spend a significant amount of time with the language and become conversational, perfecting your pronunciation can still be very challenging and take a long time.

Sure, as with any new language, the more you practice, the better your pronunciation will be. But without a very precise and thorough understanding of how each sound is made in Korean, you might still be pronouncing certain sounds incorrectly even after years of studying and speaking. And that is exactly why we made this book for you.

Think of this book as your personal pronunciation coach that will show you exactly how to pronounce each sound in Korean—what you are doing right, what you are doing wrong, and how you can make your pronunciation sound even more natural. Beginner learners can use this book as a guide to Korean pronunciation as they start learning more, and intermediate and advanced learners can use it to bridge the gap between their own pronunciation and that of a native speaker.

Ever have those moments when you know your pronunciation isn't perfectly accurate but you just don't know how to improve it? This book will give you all the necessary information to help you sound more like a native Korean speaker. Be sure to utilize all the audio and video guides provided with this book and start sounding more natural in Korean today!

CHAPTER 1.

The Pronunciation That Korean Learners Struggle with the Most: Consonants

Lesson 1 - 1

Can You Tell the Difference Between ㄱ, ㅋ, and ㄲ?

● **Read the following three characters aloud.**

Did you pronounce ㄱ, ㅋ, and ㄲ differently?

▶ **Now, listen to a native speaker's pronunciation.**
01

How did you compare? Are you able to differentiate between ㄱ, ㅋ, and ㄲ?

The position of the tongue is the same for ㄱ, ㅋ, and ㄲ. Of the three, ㅋ is pronounced with the strongest puff of air, while ㄲ is pronounced with very little air. In other words, when ㅋ is pronounced, the throat opens up the most, and when ㄲ is pronounced, the throat opens up the least.

Now, let's practice again. As above, we will practice by adding the vowel — to ㄱ, ㅋ, and ㄲ, but this time we will practice them in order starting from the sound that creates the most to the least amount of air. It is also a good idea to hold your palm in front of your mouth to feel the amount of air you produce when practicing.

● **Give it a try.**

ㅋ ㄱ ㄲ

▶ **Practice again while watching the video.**
02

Are you still having trouble differentiating between the sounds? If so, try pronouncing them with different tones.

Pronounce ㄱ with a low tone, and use a higher tone to pronounce ㅋ and ㄲ.

▶ First, listen carefully to the native speaker's pronunciation and repeat it.

Do you find ㄱ and ㅋ easy, but ㄲ difficult? If so, let's practice just ㄲ.

Place your tongue on the roof of your mouth on your palate like you are making the ㄱ sound. You can feel the back of your tongue on the roof of your mouth, right? Hold your breath while keeping it there, and after three seconds, push the back of your tongue down and release it from your palate, making a sound.

▶ Practice while watching the video.

How To Sound Like A Native Korean Speaker

▶ Now, let's practice by listening and repeating the sounds that ㄱ, ㅋ, and ㄲ
06 produce when combined with vowels other than ㅡ.

- 가 카 까 ・ 거 커 꺼

- 고 코 꼬 ・ 구 쿠 꾸

- 게 케 께 ・ 기 키 끼

Lesson 1 - 2

Are You Playing with a Ball or a Bean?

▶ Let's practice with some common everyday words, and see what can happen if we do not pronounce ㄱ, ㅋ, and ㄲ distinctly.

07 · 공 ball   · 콩 bean

08 · 곡 (a piece of) music   · 꼭 surely, at any cost

09 · 굴 oysters   · 꿀 honey

10 · 곧 soon   · 꽃 flower

11 · 기 energy   · 키 height   · 끼 counter for meals

12 · 가요. Go.   · 까요. Peel it.

13 · 가지 eggplant   · 까지 to, until

14 · 커요. It is big.   · 꺼요. Turn it off.

15 · 고리 ring, hook   · 꼬리 tail

16 · 갰어요. I folded (it) up.   · 캤어요. I dug (it) up.   · 깼어요. I broke it.

This time, we have some words containing combinations of ㄱ, ㅋ, and ㄲ.

 **Let's practice by listening to the native speaker and following along.**

17

가끔 sometimes

코끼리 elephant

코감기 sinus cold

검은깨 black sesame

코끝 the tip of one's nose

콩국수 cold bean soup noodles

꼭대기 top

가까워요. It's close.

Quiz Time!

Listen to the audio and check the box that corresponds to the correct pronunciation of the written word.

Ex1. 꿀 (= honey)   ⓐ ☑ⓑ ⓒ ⓓ

Q1. 꿈 (= dream)   ⓐ ⓑ ⓒ ⓓ

Q2. 간 (= liver)   ⓐ ⓑ ⓒ ⓓ

Q3. 감 (= persimmon)   ⓐ ⓑ ⓒ ⓓ

Q4. 칸 (= room, space)   ⓐ ⓑ ⓒ ⓓ

Q5. 칼 (= knife)   ⓐ ⓑ ⓒ ⓓ

Listen to the audio and select the consonant that goes in the blank.

Q6.

| 배 | 흡 |

(a) ㄱ　　(b) ㅋ　　(c) ㄲ

Q7.

| ㄴ | ᄅ |

(a) ㄱ　　(b) ㅋ　　(c) ㄲ

Q8.

| ㅐ | 미 |

(a) ㄱ　　(b) ㅋ　　(c) ㄲ

Q9.

| ㄷ | 아 | 들 |

(a) ㄱ　　(b) ㅋ　　(c) ㄲ

Q10.

| ㅗ | ㅜ | 마 |

(a) ㄱ　　(b) ㅋ　　(c) ㄲ

Q11.

| ㅗ | ㅣ |

(a) ㄱ　　(b) ㅋ　　(c) ㄲ

▶ Listen to the audio and number the words in the order they are said.

Ex2. 곡 (3) 콕 (2) 꼭 (1)

Q12. 기 (   ) 키 (   ) 끼 (   )

Q13. 금 (   ) 큼 (   ) 끔 (   )

Q14. 갰어요. (   ) 캤어요. (   ) 깼어요. (   )

Let's practice with sentences!

▶ This time, let's practice ㄱ, ㅋ, and ㄲ using sentences. Read the sentences below slowly, and then practice reading them faster.

Q15. **공으로 꽃병을 깼어요.**
↳ [공:으로 꼳뼝을 깨써요.]
= I broke the vase with a ball.

Q16. **이 고양이는 꼬리가 길고 키가 커요.**
= This cat has a long tail and is tall.

Q17. **코끼리는 코끝으로 굴을 까요.**
↳ [코끼리는 코끄트로 구를 까요.]
= The elephant shucks an oyster with the tip of its nose.

Q18. 산꼭대기에서 먹는 감이 꿀처럼 달아요.

↳ [산꼭때기에서 멍는 가:미 꿀처럼 다라요.]

= Persimmons eaten at the top of a mountain are as sweet as honey.

Q19. 이 검은깨 콩국수 꼭 먹어 보세요.

↳ [이 거믄깨 콩국쑤 꽁 머거 보세요.]

= You have to try these black sesame soy noodles.

Answers

Q1. ⓒ (굼쿰꿈쿰)

Q2. ⓐ (간칸깐칸)

Q3. ⓑ (캄감깜깜)

Q4. ⓓ (깐간깐칸)

Q5. ⓐ (칼깔깔갈)

Q6. ⓒ (배꼽 = navel)

Q7. ⓒ (느낌 = feeling, sense)

Q8. ⓐ (개미 = ant)

Q9. ⓑ (큰아들 = one's eldest son)

Q10. ⓐ (고구마 = sweet potato)

Q11. ⓐ (고기 = meat)

Q12. (2)-(3)-(1)

Q13. (1)-(2)-(3)

Q14. (2)-(1)-(3)

Lesson 2 - 1

Can You Tell the Difference Between ㄷ, ㅌ, and ㄸ?

● **Read the following three syllables aloud.**

Did you pronounce the three sounds 드, 트, and 뜨 differently?

(▶) **Now, listen to the native speaker's pronunciation.**
01

What do you think? Is it similar to your pronunciation? Can you differentiate between the three sounds 드, 트, and 뜨?

When you pronounce ㄷ, ㅌ, and ㄸ, the position of the tongue is the same. However, the sound you produce is different. ㅌ produces the most air of the three when pronounced. On the other hand, the sound of ㄸ produces very little air. In other words, when ㅌ is pronounced, your throat opens up the most, and when ㄸ is pronounced, your throat opens up the least.

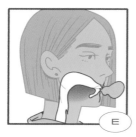
ㅌ

ㄷ

ㄸ

Now, let's practice again. As above, we will practice by adding the vowel ㅡ to ㄷ, ㅌ, and ㄸ, but this time we will practice them in order from the most to the least amount of air used. It is also a good idea to hold your palm in front of your mouth to feel the amount of air you produce when practicing.

● **Now, try for yourself.**

ㅌ ㄷ ㄸ
ㅡ ㅡ ㅡ

▶ **Practice again while watching the video.**
02

Are you still having trouble differentiating between the sounds? If so, try pronouncing them with different tones.

● Pronounce ㅌ using a low tone, and pronounce ㅌ with the highest tone of the three.

● Compare yourself with the native speaker.

03

Do you find ㄷ and ㅌ easy, but ㄸ difficult? If so, let's practice just ㄸ.

● Put the tip of your tongue firmly behind your front teeth like you are making the ㄷ sound. Hold your breath for 2-3 seconds while keeping it there. Build up air, then release your tongue, making the sound. Three, two, one, ㄸ!

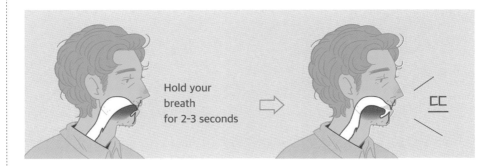

Hold your breath for 2-3 seconds

▶ Practice again while watching the video.
04

▶ Now, let's practice by listening and repeating the sounds that ㄷ, ㅌ, and ㄸ
05 make when combined with other vowels.

- 다 타 따 · 더 터 떠

- 도 토 또 · 두 투 뚜

- 데 테 떼 · 디 티 띠

How To Sound Like A Native Korean Speaker

Lesson 2 - 2

Are You Saying That You Dusted Off Your Clothes or That You Shivered?

▶ Let's practice and see what could happen if we do not differentiate ㄷ, ㅌ, and ㄸ clearly when we pronounce them.

06	· 담 wall	· 땀 sweat	
07	· 답 answer	· 탑 tower	
08	· 들 field	· 틀 cast, outline	· 뜰 yard
09	· 달 moon	· 탈 mask; trouble	· 딸 daughter
10	· 당 sugar; (political) party	· 탕 soup	· 땅 land, ground
11	· 덕 virtue	· 턱 chin	· 떡 rice cake
12	· 동 copper; east	· 통 bucket, container	· 똥 poop
13	· 들려요. I can hear it.	· 틀려요. It is wrong.	
14	· 들어요. Listen.	· 틀어요. Turn it on.	
15	· 덜었어요. I took some.	· 털었어요. I dusted.	· 떨었어요. I shivered.

This time, we have some words that use combinations of ㄷ, ㅌ, and ㄸ.

Shall we practice by listening to the native speaker and following along?

16

두통 headache

태도 attitude

뒤뚱뒤뚱 걸어요. He/she waddles.

투덜이 스머프 Grouchy Smurf

뜀틀 vaulting box

도토리 acorn

떠들어요. They talk loudly.

Quiz Time!

Listen to the audio and check the box that corresponds to the correct pronunciation of the written word.

Ex1. 땅 (= land, ground) ⓐ  ⓒ ⓓ

Q1. 더 (= more) ⓐ ⓑ ⓒ ⓓ

Q2. 돈 (= money) ⓐ ⓑ ⓒ ⓓ

Q3. 또 (= again, once more) ⓐ ⓑ ⓒ ⓓ

Q4. 틈 (= crack, gap) ⓐ ⓑ ⓒ ⓓ

Q5. 뒤 (= back) ⓐ ⓑ ⓒ ⓓ

Listen to the audio and select the consonant that goes in the blank.

Q6.

ⓐ ㄷ　ⓑ ㅌ　ⓒ ㄸ

Q7.

ⓐ ㄷ　ⓑ ㅌ　ⓒ ㄸ

Q8.

ⓐ ㄷ　ⓑ ㅌ　ⓒ ㄸ

Q9.

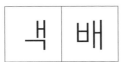

ⓐ ㄷ　ⓑ ㅌ　ⓒ ㄸ

Q10.

ⓐ ㄷ　ⓑ ㅌ　ⓒ ㄸ

Q11.

ⓐ ㄷ　ⓑ ㅌ　ⓒ ㄸ

▶ Listen to the audio and number the words in the order they are said.

Ex2. 담 (2) 탐 (1) 땀 (3)

Q12. 동 (　　) 통 (　　) 똥 (　　)

Q13. 들 (　　) 틀 (　　) 뜰 (　　)

Q14. 덜었어요. (　　) 털었어요. (　　) 떨었어요. (　　)

Let's practice with sentences!

▶ This time, let's practice ㄷ, ㅌ, and ㄸ using sentences. Read the sentences below slowly, then practice reading them again faster.

Q15. 떡이 너무 딱딱해서 턱이 아파요.
↳ [떠기 너무 딱따캐서 터기 아파요.]
= The rice cake is so hard that my jaw hurts.

Q16. 튀김 먹고 탈이 나서 땀이 났어요.
↳ [튀김 먹꼬 타:리 나서 따미 나써요.]
= I got sick from eating fried food so I was sweating.

Q17. 투덜이 스머프가 계속 떠들고 있어요.
↳ [투더리 스머프가 계:속 떠:들고 이써요.]
= Grouchy Smurf keeps talking.

How To Sound Like A Native Korean Speaker

Q18. 드디어 택배가 도착했어요.

↳ [드디어 택빼가 도:차캐써요.]

= The package finally arrived.

Q19. 당이 떨어져서 사탕 먹어야 돼요.

↳ [당이 떠러저서 사탕 머거야 돼요.]

= My blood sugar is low so I need to eat some candy.

Answers

Q1. ⓒ (떠터더터)

Q2. ⓐ (돈뜬뜬돈)

Q3. ⓐ (또토토도)

Q4. ⓑ (듬틈뜸뜸)

Q5. ⓓ (뛰뛰튀뛰)

Q6. ⓒ (때 = the time, the moment)

Q7. ⓑ (기타 = guitar; and so on)

Q8. ⓒ (따로 = separately)

Q9. ⓑ (택배 = parcel delivery service)

Q10. ⓐ (동전 = coin)

Q11. ⓐ (드디어 = at last; finally)

Q12. (1)-(2)-(3)

Q13. (1)-(3)-(2)

Q14. (2)-(1)-(3)

Lesson 3 - 1

Can You Tell the Difference Between ㅂ, ㅍ, and ㅃ?

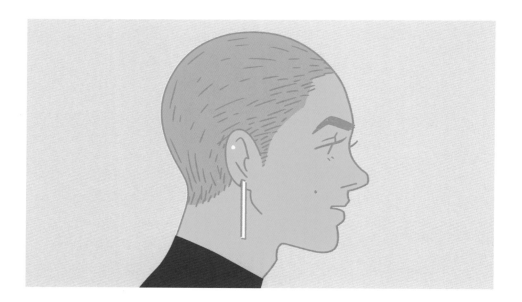

● Read these three characters aloud.

▶ Now, listen to the native speaker's pronunciation.
01

What do you think? Was your pronunciation similar?

How To Sound Like A Native Korean Speaker

ㅂ, ㅍ, and ㅃ are sounds that are made by closing your mouth and then opening your lips. Of the three, ㅍ produces the most air when pronounced, while ㅃ only produces a small amount of air. In other words, when ㅍ is pronounced, your throat opens up the most, and the most air comes out. When ㅃ is pronounced, your throat opens up the least, and the least amount of air is released.

Now, let's practice again. As above, try to pronounce the syllables by adding the ㅡ vowel to ㅂ, ㅍ, and ㅃ. We will practice them in order starting from the most to the least amount of air produced. It is also a good idea to hold your palm in front of your mouth to feel the amount of air you produce when practicing.

● **Now, try for yourself.**

프   브   쁘

▶ **Practice again while watching the video.**
02

Are you still having trouble differentiating between the sounds? If so, try pronouncing them with different tones.

- Try pronouncing ㅂ using a low tone, and ㅍ using a high tone.

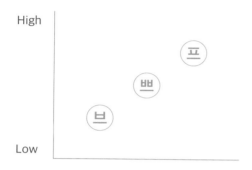

High

Low

▶ Compare yourself with the native speaker.
03

Are ㅂ and ㅍ easy, but ㅃ is difficult?

- Try to purse your lips tightly. Then, build up air behind your lips for 2-3 seconds. Finally, release while making the sound. Three, two, one, ㅃ!

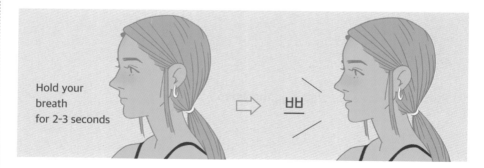

Hold your breath for 2-3 seconds

ㅃ

▶ Compare yourself with the native speaker's pronunciation.
04

▶ Now, let's practice by listening and repeating the sounds that ㅂ, ㅍ, and ㅃ
05 make when combined with other vowels.

- 바 파 빠 · 버 퍼 뻐
- 보 포 뽀 · 부 푸 뿌
- 베 페 뻬 · 비 피 삐

Lesson 3 -2

Do You Feel Pain in Your Foot or in Your Arm?

▶ Let's practice and see what could happen if we do not differentiate clearly between ㅂ, ㅍ, and ㅃ when pronouncing them.

06	• 발 foot	• 팔 arm; eight		
07	• 비 rain	• 피 blood	• 삐 beep	
08	• 방 room	• 빵 bread		
09	• 백 hundred	• 팩 face mask		
10	• 불 fire, light	• 풀 grass; glue; swimming pool	• 뿔 horn	
11	• 발리 Bali	• 빨리 quickly		
12	• 비자 visa	• 피자 pizza		
13	• 팬티 underpants	• 벤티 Venti (drink size)		
14	• 팔아요? Do you sell it?	• 빨아요? Do you wash it?		
15	• 변했어요. It has changed.	• 편했어요. It was comfortable.		

This time, we have some words that contain combinations of ㅂ, ㅍ, and ㅃ.

 **Shall we practice by listening to the native speaker and following along?**

16

피부 skin   반팔 short-sleeved shirt

발표 announcement; presentation   보풀 fluff (= 보푸라기)

팥빵 red bean bread   배고파요. I am hungry.

바빠요. I am busy.   평범해요. It's plain/common/typical/normal.

Quiz Time!

Listen to the audio and check the box that corresponds to the correct pronunciation of the written word.

Ex1. 발 (= foot)   ⓐ ✔ⓑ ⓒ ⓓ

Q1. 표 (= ticket; table)   ⓐ ⓑ ⓒ ⓓ

Q2. 밥 (= meal, cooked rice)   ⓐ ⓑ ⓒ ⓓ

Q3. 별 (= star)   ⓐ ⓑ ⓒ ⓓ

Q4. 뼈 (= bone)   ⓐ ⓑ ⓒ ⓓ

Q5. 밤 (= night)   ⓐ ⓑ ⓒ ⓓ

Listen to the audio and choose which consonant goes in the blank. When you have finished answering all the questions, read along while you listen again.

Q6.

┌───┬───┐
│ ㅜ │ 리 │
└───┴───┘

(a) ㅂ   (b) ㅍ   (c) ㅃ

Q7.

┌───┬───┐
│ ᅴ │ 써 │
└───┴───┘

(a) ㅂ   (b) ㅍ   (c) ㅃ

Q8.

┌───┬───┐
│ ㅜ │ ㅜ │
└───┴───┘

(a) ㅂ   (b) ㅍ   (c) ㅃ

Q9.

┌───┬───┐
│ ㅗ │ 장 │
└───┴───┘

(a) ㅂ   (b) ㅍ   (c) ㅃ

Q10.

┌───┬───┐
│ ᅧᆼ │ 균 │
└───┴───┘

(a) ㅂ   (b) ㅍ   (c) ㅃ

Q11.

┌───┬───┐
│ 신 │ ᅡᆯ │
└───┴───┘

(a) ㅂ   (b) ㅍ   (c) ㅃ

How To Sound Like A Native Korean Speaker

Ex2. 발 (3) 팔 (2) 빨 (1)

Q12. 비 (   ) 피 (   ) 삐 (   )

Q13. 불 (   ) 풀 (   ) 뿔 (   )

Q14. 벼 (   ) 펴 (   ) 뼈 (   )

Let's practice with sentences!

This time, let's practice ㅂ, ㅍ, and ㅃ using sentences. Read the sentences below slowly, then practice reading them again faster.

Q15. 오늘 발표할 때 팔이 너무 아팠어요.
↳ [오늘 발표할 때 파리 너무 아파써요.]
= My arm hurt so much during the presentation today.

Q16. 피자 한 판 빨리 포장해 주세요.
= Please hurry and give me one pizza to go.

Q17. 저희 부부가 결혼한 지 벌써 백 일 됐어요.
↳ [저히 부부가 결혼한 지 벌써 배길 돼써요.]
= It's already been 100 days since we became a married couple.

Q18. 이 신발 신으면 발이 편해요.

↳ [이 신발 시느면 바리 편해요.]

= If you wear these shoes, your feet will be comfortable.

Q19. 바빠서 밥을 못 먹었더니 너무 배고파요.

↳ [바빠서 바블 몬머걷떠니 너무 배고파요.]

= Because I was so busy, I didn't eat and I'm so hungry.

Answers

Q1. ⓓ (뵤뵤뾰表)

Q2. ⓐ (밥팝빱팝)

Q3. ⓒ (뻘펄벌뻘)

Q4. ⓐ (뼈펴벼펴)

Q5. ⓐ (밤팜빰팜)

Q6. ⓒ (뿌리 = root)

Q7. ⓐ (벌써 = already)

Q8. ⓐ (부부 = married couple)

Q9. ⓑ (포장 = packaging; gift-wrapping)

Q10. ⓑ (평균 = average)

Q11. ⓐ (신발 = shoes)

Q12. (2)-(1)-(3)

Q13. (1)-(2)-(3)

Q14. (1)-(2)-(3)

Lesson 4 - 1

Can You Tell the Difference Between ㅅ and ㅆ?

● **Read the following two syllables aloud.**

Did you pronounce the two sounds, 스 and 쓰, differently?

▶ **Now, listen to the native speaker's pronunciation.**

01

What do you think? Is it similar to your pronunciation? Can you differentiate

between the ㅅ sound and the ㅆ sound?

When you pronounce ㅅ and ㅆ, the position of your tongue is the same. However, the sound is different. The reason for this is because when ㅅ is pronounced, your tongue is relaxed, but when ㅆ is pronounced, your tongue and throat are tensed.

● **Shall we try pronouncing them again?**

▶ **Compare yourself with the native speaker's pronunciation.**
02

Are you still having trouble? If so, try pronouncing them with different tones.

▶ **Try pronouncing ㅅ with a low tone, and ㅆ with a higher tone. First, listen**
03 **carefully to the native speaker's pronunciation and then try to repeat it.**

Are you having trouble with the tones as well? Then we'll give you another tip.

When you pronounce a syllable that starts with ㅅ, think about first pronouncing ㅅ, followed slowly by the vowel sound. Conversely, when you pronounce a syllable that starts with ㅆ, think of pronouncing ㅆ and the vowel sound almost simultaneously.

▶ **Let's practice with 사 and 싸.**
04

사 싸

▶ **Good. Which tip helped you the most? With that tip in mind, let's pronounce**
05 **the syllables below.**

- 서　써
- 소　쏘
- 수　쑤
- 세　쎄
- 시　씨

Did you notice that ㅅ sounds different in 시, compared to how ㅅ sounds when it appears with other vowels? Do not worry about it for now. You will learn about the different sounds of ㅅ in Chapter 7 Lesson 5, "ㅅ the Chameleon".

Lesson 4 - 2

Do You Want Me to Buy It or Wrap It?

▶ Let's practice and see what could happen if we don't differentiate between ㅅ and ㅆ clearly when we pronounce them.

06 · 삼 three; ginseng   · 쌈 lettuce wrap

07 · 산 mountain   · 싼 cheap

08 · 살 flesh; fat   · 쌀 rice

09 · 상 prize; reward   · 쌍 pair

10 · 샀어요. I bought it.   · 쌌어요. It was cheap. / I wrapped it.

11 · 서요. Stand up.   · 써요. It's bitter. / Write it.

12 · 시 poem   · 씨 seed

How To Sound Like A Native Korean Speaker

This time, we have some words that use combinations of ㅅ and ㅆ.

Shall we practice by listening to the native speaker and following along?

13

새싹 sprout

상추쌈 lettuce wrap

쌍시옷 the name of the consonant "ㅆ"

싼 신발 cheap shoes

솜씨 skill

석진 씨 formal way to address a person named Seokjin

시작했어요. [시:자캐써요] I started. / It started.

Quiz Time!

Listen to the audio and check the box that corresponds to the correct pronunciation of the written word.

Ex1. 쌀 (= rice)   ⓑ

Q1. 섬 (= island)　　　　　　ⓐ　ⓑ

Q2. 속 (= the inside)　　　　ⓐ　ⓑ

Q3. 실 (= thread)　　　　　　ⓐ　ⓑ

Q4. 숲 (= forest)　　　　　　ⓐ　ⓑ

Q5. 손 (= hand)　　　　　　ⓐ　ⓑ

▶ Listen to the audio and choose which consonant goes in the blank. After answering all the questions, listen again and read along.

Q6.

ㅗ	ㅓ

ⓐ ㅅ　ⓑ ㅆ

Q7.

ㅎ	공

ⓐ ㅅ　ⓑ ㅆ

Q8.

ㅡ	레	기

ⓐ ㅅ　ⓑ ㅆ

Q9.

날	ㅣ

ⓐ ㅅ　ⓑ ㅆ

Q10.

ㅜ	건

ⓐ ㅅ　ⓑ ㅆ

Q11.

훨	ㄴㅣ

ⓐ ㅅ　ⓑ ㅆ

Ex2. 여기에 서요. (1)

여기에 써요. (2)

Q12. 이거 사 주세요. (= Please buy me this.) (   )

이거 싸 주세요. (= Please wrap this.) (   )

Q13. 좀 살살 해요. (= Be gentle.) (   )

좀 쌀쌀해요. (= It's a little chilly.) (   )

Q14. 씻었어요. (= I washed up.) (   )

시 썼어요. (= I wrote a poem.) (   )

Let's practice with sentences!

This time, let's practice ㅅ and ㅆ using sentences. Read the sentences below slowly, then practice reading them again faster.

Q15. **살이 빠져서 새 옷을 샀어요.**

↳ [사리 빠:저서 새 오슬 사써요.]

= I lost weight and bought new clothes.

Q16. **상추로 쌈을 싸서 입에 쏙!**

↳ [상추로 싸믈 싸서 이베 쏙!]

= Wrap it in lettuce and fit it in your mouth.

Q17. 싼 신발 사서 4년 신었어요.

↪ [싼 신발 사서 사: 년 시너써요.]

= I bought cheap shoes and wore them for four years.

Q18. '쌀'과 '쌍'은 쌍시옷으로 시작해요.

↪ [쌀과 쌍은 쌍시오스로 시:자캐요.]

= 'Rice' and 'pair' start with ㅆ.

Q19. 석진 씨, 이 수건 사 주세요.

↪ [석찐 씨, 이 수:건 사 주세요.]

= Seokjin, please buy me this towel.

Answers

Q1. ⓑ (썸섬)

Q2. ⓐ (속쏙)

Q3. ⓐ (실씰)

Q4. ⓑ (쑥숲)

Q5. ⓐ (손쏜)

Q6. ⓐ (소식 = news)

Q7. ⓐ (성공 = success)

Q8. ⓑ (쓰레기 = trash)

Q9. ⓑ (날씨 = weather)

Q10. ⓐ (수건 = towel)

Q11. ⓑ (훨씬 = much [more])

Q12. (1)-(2)

Q13. (2)-(1)

Q14. (2)-(1) (시 썼어요[시 써써요]-
씻었어요[씨서써요])

Can You Tell the Difference Between ㅈ, ㅊ, and ㅉ?

● **Read these three characters aloud.**

▶ **Now, listen to a native speaker's pronunciation.**

01   What do you think? Was your pronunciation similar?

When pronouncing ㅈ, ㅊ and ㅉ, the position of your tongue is the same.

Among these three, ㅊ produces the strongest puff of air when pronounced. ㅉ on the other hand, produces almost no air. When pronouncing ㅊ, your throat opens up the widest, and when pronouncing ㅉ, your throat is closed.

Let's practice again. Just like we did above, we are going to pronounce ㅈ, ㅊ, and ㅉ with the ㅡ vowel attached. We will practice them in order starting from the most to the least amount of air produced. It is also a good idea to hold your palm in front of your mouth when practicing to feel the amount of air you produce.

● **Now, try for yourself.**

▶ **Practice again while watching the video.**
02

Still not getting it? If so, try thinking of them as each having a different pitch.

● **Try pronouncing them again, with 즈 having the lowest pitch and 츠 having the highest pitch.**

▶ Compare your pronunciation with a native speaker.

You might be finding ㅈ and ㅊ easy, but what about ㅉ?

● For ㅉ, try pressing your tongue to the roof of your mouth. Let air build up behind your tongue for 2-3 seconds before releasing it and making the sound.

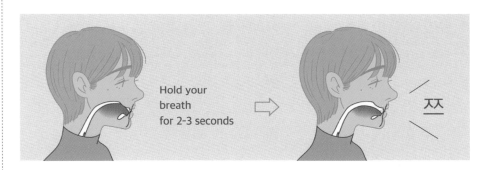

Hold your breath for 2-3 seconds   ⇨   ㅉ

▶ Practice while watching the video.

▶ Now, let's practice listening to and repeating the following syllables for ㅈ, ㅊ and ㅉ that use vowels other than ㅡ.

· 자 차 짜 · 저 처 쩌

· 조 초 쪼 · 주 추 쭈

· 제 체 쩨 · 지 치 찌

Lesson 5 - 2

Are You Asking for My Car or My Ruler?

▶ Let's practice some words that could get you into a confusing situation if you don't properly pronounce ㅈ, ㅊ, and ㅉ.

06	· 자 ruler	· 차 car; tea	
07	· 짐 burden, load	· 침 saliva; acupuncture	· 찜 steamed dish
08	· 가자. Let's go.	· 가짜 fake	
09	· 자요. Sleep.	· 차요. Kick.	· 짜요. It's salty.
10	· 자장 a magnetic field	· 차장 deputy chief	· 짜장 black bean sauce
11	· 주워요. Pick it up.	· 추워요. It's cold.	

This time, we have some words that use different combinations of ㅈ, ㅊ, and ㅉ within them.

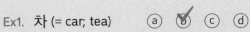 **Let's listen to a native speaker and repeat the words aloud.**

12

진짜 really, truly

주차장 parking lot

찜질방 public bathhouse, sauna

짜증 나. It's annoying.

자동차 car

짜장면 jjajangmyeon (black bean noodles)

지하철 subway

Quiz Time!

Listen to the audio and check the box that corresponds to the correct pronunciation of the word.

Ex1. 차 (= car; tea)　　ⓐ　ⓥ̌　ⓒ　ⓓ

Q1. 죽 (= porridge)　　ⓐ　ⓑ　ⓒ　ⓓ

Q2. 천 (= thousand)　　ⓐ　ⓑ　ⓒ　ⓓ

Q3. 집 (= house)　　ⓐ　ⓑ　ⓒ　ⓓ

Q4. 쪽 (= page)　　ⓐ　ⓑ　ⓒ　ⓓ

Q5. 칠 (= seven)　　ⓐ　ⓑ　ⓒ　ⓓ

Listen to the word and choose the correct consonant.

Q6.

| ㅣ | 마 |

ⓐ ㅈ   ⓑ ㅊ   ⓒ ㅉ

Q7.

| ㅗ | 구 |

ⓐ ㅈ   ⓑ ㅊ   ⓒ ㅉ

Q8.

| ㅣ | 금 |

ⓐ ㅈ   ⓑ ㅊ   ⓒ ㅉ

Q9.

| ㅣ | 개 |

ⓐ ㅈ   ⓑ ㅊ   ⓒ ㅉ

Q10.

| ㅜ | ㅓ |

ⓐ ㅈ   ⓑ ㅊ   ⓒ ㅉ

Q11.

| 왼 | ㅎ |

ⓐ ㅈ   ⓑ ㅊ   ⓒ ㅉ

▶ Listen to the audio and number the words in the order they are said.

Ex2. 장 (3) 창 (2) 짱 (1)

Q12. 자장 (   ) 차장 (   ) 짜장 (   )

Q13. 짐 (   ) 침 (   ) 찜 (   )

Q14. 자요. (   ) 차요. (   ) 짜요. (   )

Let's practice with sentences!

▶ Now, practice pronouncing ㅈ, ㅊ, ㅉ with the sentences below. Read the sentences slowly, then try reading them again faster.

Q15. 차 한 잔 주세요.

= Please give me a cup of tea.

Q16. 지난주는 좀 추웠어요.

↳ [지난주는 좀 추워써요.]

= Last week, it was a bit cold.

Q17. 이 집 짜장면 좀 짜네요.

= The jjajangmyeon here is a bit salty.

Q18. 주연이 때문에 진짜 짜증 나.

↳ [주여니 때무네 진짜 짜증 나.]

= I am so annoyed because of Jooyeon.

Q19. 제 차는 주차장 칠 층에 있어요.

↳ [제 차는 주:차장 칠 층에 이써요.]

= My car is on the seventh floor of the parking lot.

Answers

Q1. ⓒ (축쭉죽축)

Q2. ⓓ (쩐전전천)

Q3. ⓑ (칩집찝칩)

Q4. ⓓ (촉족족쪽)

Q5. ⓐ (칠찔질찔)

Q6. ⓑ (치마 = skirt)

Q7. ⓑ (친구 = friend)

Q8. ⓐ (지금 = now)

Q9. ⓒ (찌개 = stew)

Q10. ⓑ (추천 = recommendation)

Q11. ⓒ (왼쪽 = the left side)

Q12. (1)-(3)-(2)

Q13. (2)-(1)-(3)

Q14. (2)-(3)-(1)

Real Experiences by Korean Learners

This anecdote shared by Tofu2020, USA

I tried to order a coffee but accidentally said 코피 instead of 커피.

I certainly did not want to order a nosebleed!

CHAPTER 2.

The Pronunciation That Korean Learners Struggle with the Most: Vowels

Lesson 1 - 1

Can You Pronounce 오 and 어 Differently?

● **Please read 오어 and 어오 aloud.**

오어   어오

Can you pronounce the difference between 오 and 어 clearly?

▶ **Listen to the native speaker's pronunciation.**
01

How was it? When listening, do 오 and 어 clearly sound different?
In this lesson, let's practice the pronunciation of 오 and 어.

▶ **When pronouncing 오 and 어, first look at the difference in the shape of your**
02 **mouth.**

오

어

As you can see in the picture above, when 오 is pronounced, the lips are rounded and pushed out. When 어 is pronounced, the jaw is lowered and the mouth opens in a triangular shape.

● Let's repeat the two vowels again. When you pronounce 오, raise your jaw and stick out your lips more than when pronouncing 어. When you pronounce 어, lower your jaw more than when pronouncing 오. If you are unsure of what this means, try practicing while watching the video.

03

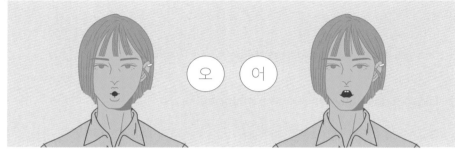

04

How To Sound Like A Native Korean Speaker

▶ Did you practice enough? Now, let's practice by putting various consonants in
05 front of the vowels ㅗ and ㅓ. Listen and repeat.

- 고 거 코 커
- 노 너 도 더 토 터
- 소 서 로 러 호 허
- 모 머 보 버 포 퍼
- 조 저 초 처

Lesson 1 - 2

A Cup of Nosebleed in the Morning?

If you pronounce 커피 (coffee), the thing we drink, with ㅗ instead of ㅓ by mistake, you will say 코피, and the meaning changes to "nosebleed". "Coffee" and "nosebleed" have two very different meanings, right? For this reason, pronouncing ㅗ and ㅓ properly is important.

▶ Let's look at some other words used in everyday life that include ㅗ and ㅓ.

06	• 소 bull; cow	• 서! Stop (walking)!
07	• 손 hand	• 선 line
08	• 솔 brush	• 설 Lunar New Year's Day
09	• 좀 a little	• 점 dot; point
10	• 곳 place	• 것 thing
11	• 코피 nosebleed	• 커피 coffee
12	• 고리 ring; loop	• 거리 street; road; avenue
13	• 볼래. I want to see it.	• 벌레 worm; bug
14	• 오이없어요. There is no cucumber.	• 어이없어요. I am dumbfounded.
15	• 조금 a little	• 저금 saving; savings

How To Sound Like A Native Korean Speaker

In the following examples, both ㅗ and ㅓ are used in one word.

Listen and practice repeating the native speaker's pronunciation.

16

오징어 squid

오전 morning; a.m.

조언 advice

청소 cleaning

놀이터 playground

서로 each other

전공 major

종이컵 paper cup

Quiz Time!

Choose whether the native speaker said the fifth syllable as 오 or 어.

Ex1.   ○ ○ ○ ○ ●
◀)) 어 어 오 오 오   ☑ⓐ오   ⓑ어

Q1. ○ ○ ○ ○ ●
    ⓐ오   ⓑ어

Q2. ○ ○ ○ ○ ●
    ⓐ오   ⓑ어

Q3. ○ ○ ○ ○ ●
    ⓐ오   ⓑ어

Q4. ○ ○ ○ ○ ●
    ⓐ오   ⓑ어

▶ Listen to the audio and choose the word that was said twice.

Ex2. ● ● ○
◀» 코 코 커   ✓ⓐ 코 ⓑ 커

Q5. ⓐ 좀 ⓑ 점   Q6. ⓐ 손 ⓑ 선   Q7. ⓐ 곳 ⓑ 것

▶ Check the box that corresponds to the correct pronunciation of the written word.

Ex3. 너도 (= you also...)   ✓ⓐ ◀» 너도 ⓑ ◀» 노도

Q8. 자전거 (= bicycle)   ⓐ   ⓑ

Q9. 바로 (= immediately)   ⓐ   ⓑ

Q10. 사고 (= accident)   ⓐ   ⓑ

Q11. 먼저 (= earlier, first)   ⓐ   ⓑ

Q12. 건조기 (= dryer, drying machine)   ⓐ   ⓑ   ⓒ

Let's practice with sentences!

▶ This time, we will practice using ㅗ and ㅓ in sentences. Please read the sentences below slowly. Then practice reading them again faster and faster.

Q13. 커피 좀 더 주세요.

= Please give me some more coffee.

Q14. 자전거 타는 거 좋아해?

↳ [자전거 타는 거 조:아해?]

= Do you like bike riding?

Q15. 너 먼저 가. 나도 바로 갈게.

↳ [너 먼저 가. 나도 바로 갈께.]

= You go first. I'll be right behind you.

Q16. 저금 조금밖에 못 했어요.

↳ [저:금 조금바께 모:태써요.]

= I was only able to save a little money.

Q17. 서로 먼저 가려다가 사고 났어요.

↳ [서로 먼저 가려다가 사:고 나써요.]

= They both tried to go first and got in an accident.

Answers

Q1. ⓐ (어어어어오)	Q5. ⓐ (좀좀점)	Q9. ⓑ (바러-바로)
Q2. ⓑ (오오오오어)	Q6. ⓐ (손선손)	Q10. ⓐ (사고-사거)
Q3. ⓑ (어오어오어)	Q7. ⓑ (것것곳)	Q11. ⓐ (먼저-몬조)
Q4. ⓐ (오어오어오)	Q8. ⓐ (자전거-자존고)	Q12. ⓑ (건저기-**건조기**-곤저기)

Lesson 2 - 1

Can You Pronounce 요 and 여 Differently?

- Please read 요여 and 여요 aloud.

요여   여요

Can you clearly pronounce 요 and 여 differently?

▶ **Listen to the native speaker's pronunciation.**
01

How was it? When listening, did 요 and 여 sound different?

If it was difficult to clearly distinguish between 요 and 여, let's practice the pronunciation in this lesson.

First, you can think of 요 as 이오 pronounced quickly. In other words, you can make the sound by quickly changing from the 이 mouth shape to the 오 mouth shape.

▶ **Watch the video, and try following along.**
02

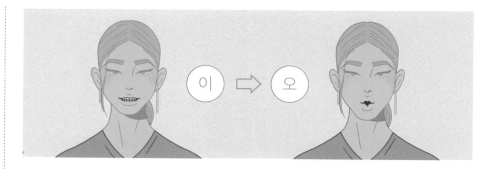

How To Sound Like A Native Korean Speaker

You can think of 여 as 이어 being pronounced quickly. In other words, you can make the sound by quickly changing from the 이 mouth shape to the 어 mouth shape.

▶ **Watch the video, and try following along.**
03

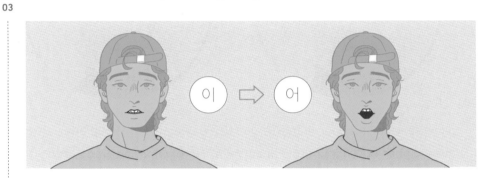

▶ **Shall we try repeating the two vowels again?**
04

When 오 and 어 are pronounced in succession, the jaw merely needs to be lowered from the mouth shape of 오 to pronounce 어. However, when 요 and 여 are pronounced in succession, you must make the 이 mouth shape first before lowering your jaw and pronouncing 여.

여

요

Likewise, when pronouncing 어오, you first pronounce 어, and then raise your jaw and push out your lips to pronounce 오. However, when pronouncing 여 before moving to 요, you must first extend the corners of your mouth out long before pushing out and rounding your lips.

● **Follow along while paying attention to the shape of the mouth in the video.**

06 **Did you practice enough? Now, let's practice by putting various consonants in front of the vowels ㅛ and ㅕ. Listen and repeat.**

• 교 겨 쿄 커

• 뇨 녀 됴 뎌 툐 텨

• 료 려

• 묘 며 뵤 벼 표 펴

- 쇼 셔
- 효 혀

Lesson 2 - 2

Is It Yoga Time or Free Time?

In truth, Koreans often pronounce 요 as 여. For example, it is not uncommon for people to pronounce words like 아니요 as 아니여 or 맞아요 as 맞아여. However, it is not always possible or correct to pronounce ㅛ like ㅕ all the time. This is because sometimes a difference in pronunciation can cause the entire meaning of the word to change.

▶ Shall we take a look at how the meaning changes when ㅛ is pronounced as ㅕ or when ㅕ is pronounced as ㅛ?

07	· 용 dragon	· 영 zero
08	· 욕 swear word, curse	· 역 station
09	· 용어 term; terminology	· 영어 English
10	· 요가 시간 yoga session	· 여가 시간 leisure time; spare time
11	· 표 주세요. Please give me a ticket.	· 펴 주세요. Please spread it out.
12	· 긴 요정 long fairy; long elf	· 긴 여정 long journey; long itinerary
13	· 수용할 수 있어요. It can accommodate; I can accept it.	· 수영할 수 있어요. I can swim.

This time, ㅗ and ㅕ are used together in one word or expression.

▶ Listen and practice along with the native speaker.

14

표현 expression; representation

형용사 adjective

별표 asterisk

셔요. It is sour.

버렸어요. I threw it away.

당연하죠. Of course. (* 죠 can be pronounced as 조.)

어려워요. It is difficult.

기다려요. I am waiting; Wait.

Quiz Time!

▶ Choose whether the native speaker said the fifth word as 요 or 여.

Ex1. ○ ○ ○ ○ ●
🔊 여 여 요 요 요

ⓐ 요   ⓑ 여

Q1. ○ ○ ○ ○ ●
　　ⓐ 요   ⓑ 여

Q2. ○ ○ ○ ○ ●
　　ⓐ 요   ⓑ 여

Q3. ○ ○ ○ ○ ●
　　ⓐ 요   ⓑ 여

Q4. ○ ○ ○ ○ ●
　　ⓐ 요   ⓑ 여

▶ Listen to the audio and choose the word that was said twice.

Ex2. ● ● ○
🔊 쿄 쿄 켜   ⓐ✓ 쿄 ⓑ 켜

Q5. ⓐ 용 ⓑ 영

Q6. ⓐ 표 ⓑ 펴

Q7. ⓐ 욕 ⓑ 역

▶ Mark the circle where the given word is said.

Ex3. 영어 (= English)   ✓ 🔊 영어 ⓑ 🔊 용어

Q8. 비교 (= comparison)   ⓐ ⓑ

Q9. 겨우 (= barely)   ⓐ ⓑ

Q10. 목표 (= target; goal)   ⓐ ⓑ

Q11. 별명 (= nickname)   ⓐ ⓑ

Q12. 내려요. (= I am getting off.)   ⓐ ⓑ ⓒ

Let's practice with sentences!

(▶) This time, we will practice ㅛ and ㅕ in sentences. Please read the sentences below slowly. Then practice by reading them again faster and faster.

Q13. 여가 시간에 저는 주로 요가원에 가요.

　↪ [여가 시가네 저는 주로 요가워네 가요.]

= In my spare time, I usually go to yoga.

Q14. '명사', '형용사', 문법 용어가 너무 어려워요.

　↪ [명사, 형용사, 문뻡 용:어가 너무 어려워요.]

= Grammar terms like "nouns" and "adjectives" are so difficult.

Q15. 저는 수영을 잘해서 별명이 물개예요.

　↪ [저는 수영을 잘해서 별명이 물깨예요.]

= I am good at swimming, so my nickname is Seal.

Q16. 역에서 표 먼저 사고 기다려요.

　↪ [여게서 표 먼저 사고 기다려요.]

= Buy a ticket at the station first and wait.

Q17. 이 영어 표현에 왜 별표 쳤어요?

　↪ [이 영어 표혀네 왜 별:표 처써요*?] * 쳐 is pronounced as 처.

= Why did you put a star on this English expression?

Answers

Q1. ⓑ (요요요요여)	Q5. ⓐ (용영용)	Q9. ⓑ (교우-겨우)
Q2. ⓐ (여여여여요)	Q6. ⓑ (표펴펴)	Q10. ⓐ (목표-먹펴)
Q3. ⓑ (여요여요여)	Q7. ⓑ (역욕역)	Q11. ⓐ (별명-볼묭)
Q4. ⓐ (요여요여요)	Q8. ⓑ (비겨-비교)	Q12. ⓑ (내료요-내려료-내료여)

Lesson 3 - 1

Can You Pronounce 으 and 어 Differently?

● **Please read 으어 and 어으 aloud.**

으어   어으

 Now, listen to the native speaker's pronunciation.
01

What do you think? Can you tell the difference between the two vowels clearly?

If the pronunciation of 으 and 어 sound similar to you, or if they were difficult for you to pronounce, use this lesson to sharpen your skills.

▶ **Let's look at how the shape of the mouth differs when pronouncing 으 versus 어.**
02

으

어

As seen in the picture above, when 으 is pronounced, your lips are open with the upper and lower teeth only slightly visible. When 어 is pronounced, your lips are open about 1 cm. When you pronounce 으, the shape of your mouth is flat. When you pronounce 어, the shape of your mouth is rounded and smaller than when you pronounce 아.

● **Shall we try practicing the two vowels in succession? Try to pay attention to the shape of the mouth in the video.**

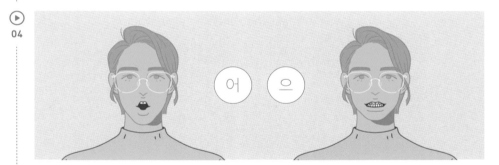

▶ **Did you practice enough? Now let's practice by putting various consonants in front of the vowels — and ㅓ. Listen and repeat.**
05

· 그 거 크 커

- 느 너 드 더 트 터
- 스 서 르 러 흐 허
- 므 머 브 버 프 퍼
- 즈 저 츠 처

Lesson 3 - 2

Did You Get It Wrong or Were You Robbed?

▶ Shall we look at some cases where the meaning changes completely when
— is pronounced like ㅓ and vice versa?

06	• 금 gold	• 검 sword
07	• 틀 frame	• 털 hair, fur
08	• 금지 prohibition, ban	• 검지 index finger
09	• 데이트 date	• 데이터 data
10	• 들어요. Listen. / Lift it up.	• 덜어요. Take some (out).
11	• 틀었어요. I turned it on.	• 털었어요. I dusted (it off).
12	• 틀렸어요. I got it wrong.	• 털렸어요. I was robbed.
13	• 늘었어요. It has increased. / It has improved.	• 널었어요 I have hung it.

In the following examples, both — and ㅓ are used in one word.

▶ **Practice by listening to and repeating the native speaker's pronunciation.**

14

그거 the thing   어느 which

처음 first   근처 vicinity

전등 light; light bulb   서른 thirty

얼음 ice   그러면 if so, then

Quiz Time!

▶ Choose whether the native speaker said the fifth word as 으 or 어.

Ex1. ○ ○ ○ ○ ●
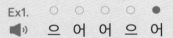

Q1. ○ ○ ○ ○ ●   Q2. ○ ○ ○ ○ ●
　　ⓐ 으 ⓑ 어   　　ⓐ 으 ⓑ 어

Q3. ○ ○ ○ ○ ●   Q4. ○ ○ ○ ○ ●
　　ⓐ 으 ⓑ 어   　　ⓐ 으 ⓑ 어

▶ Listen to the audio and choose the word that was said twice.

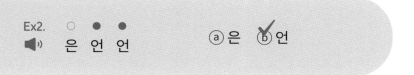

Ex2.
🔊 　○ ● ●
　　은 언 언　　　　ⓐ 은　✓ⓑ 언

Q5. ⓐ 금　ⓑ 검　　　　Q6. ⓐ 틀　ⓑ 털　　　　Q7. ⓐ 금지　ⓑ 검지

▶ Listen to the audio and connect the consonants and vowels to complete the word.

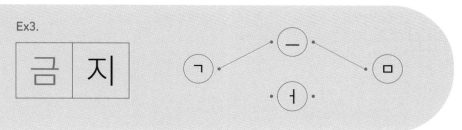

Ex3.

금 지

Q8.

림

Q9.

의

Q10.

Q11.

Q12.

Let's practice with sentences!

▶ This time, we will practice ― and ㅓ in sentences. Please read the sentences below slowly. Then practice by reading them again faster and faster.

Q13. 물을 틀었는데 얼음처럼 차가워요.

↳ [무를 트런는데 어름처럼 차가워요.]

= I turned on the water, and it is as cold as ice.

Q14. 트림 금지. 더러워요.

= No burping. That's dirty.

Q15. 제가 한국어 하는 거 들었어요?

↳ [제가 한ː구거 하는 거 드러써요?]

= Did you hear me speaking Korean?

Q16. 그러면 은희 씨 서른 넘었어요?

↳ [그러면 은히 씨 서른 너머써요?]

= So, Eunhee is over thirty?

Q17. 설마 석진 씨 그거 틀렸어요?

↳ [설마 석찐 씨 그거 틀려써요?]

= Seokjin, you couldn't possibly have gotten that wrong, right?

Answers

Q1. ⓐ (어어어으)	Q7. ⓑ (검지-검지-금지)
Q2. ⓑ (어으으으어)	Q8. 트림 (= burp; belching; eructation)
Q3. ⓑ (으으어으어)	Q9. 거의 (= almost)
Q4. ⓐ (으어으어으)	Q10. 가을 (= fall)
Q5. ⓑ (금검검)	Q11. 설마 (= No way; I doubt that.)
Q6. ⓐ (틀털틀)	Q12. 모든 (= all, every)

Lesson 4 - 1

Can You Pronounce 우 and 으 Differently?

● Please read 우으 and 으우 aloud.

우으   으우

(▶) Now, listen to the native speaker's pronunciation.
01

What do you think? Can you tell the difference between the two vowels clearly?

If the pronunciation of 우 and 으 sounded similar, or if it was difficult to pronounce them, then continue practicing with this lesson.

(▶) We will first look at how the shape of the mouth is different when
02 pronouncing 우 versus 으.

As shown in the picture above, when 우 is pronounced, the lips are gathered in a circle and pushed out. When 으 is pronounced, the lips are flat. When 우 is pronounced, the rounded lips should be lifted slightly toward the nose, and when 으 is pronounced, the lower lip should be lowered and flattened so that the lower teeth are visible. However, the position of the lower jaw when you pronounce both 우 and 으 is almost the same.

- **Shall we try the two vowels again? When you practice, listen not only to how the native speaker pronounces the vowels, but also watch how the shape of the mouth in the video changes from 우 to 으 or from 으 to 우 and try to copy it.**

03

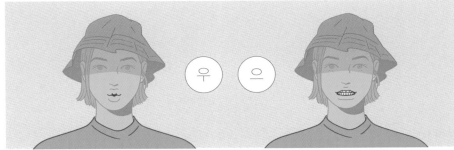

04

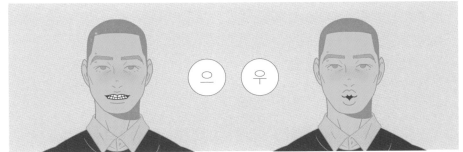

▶ 05 Did you practice enough? Now let's try pronouncing the vowels ㅜ and ㅡ with various consonants in front of them. Listen and repeat.

- 구 그 쿠 크
- 누 느 두 드 투 트
- 수 스 루 르 후 흐
- 무 므 부 브 푸 프
- 주 즈 추 츠

How To Sound Like A Native Korean Speaker

Lesson 4 - 2

Are You Saying That You Are Lucky or That You Like Silver?

▶ Let's take a look at some examples where the meaning of a word completely changes when ㅜ is pronounced like ㅡ, or when ㅡ is pronounced like ㅜ.

06
· 운이 좋아요.
I am lucky.

· 은이 좋아요.
I like silver.

07
· 굵어요. [굴:거요.]
It's thick.

· 긁어요. [글거요.]
I scratch.

08
· 그분
the person

· 구분
separation; classification

· 구 분
nine minutes

09
· 아이 둘
two children

· 아이들
children

10
· 군대
military

· 근데
by the way, but

11
· 글
writing; text

· 굴
oyster

12
· 구만
ninety thousand

· 그만!
Stop!

Now, we will look at some words containing both ㅜ and ㅡ.

Listen to the native speaker's pronunciation and practice.

13

구름 cloud   무릎 knee

스물 twenty   불가능해요. It's impossible.

부끄러워요. I feel shy.   부드러워요. It's soft.

그만둘 거예요. I'm going to quit.

서두르지 마세요. Don't rush.

Quiz Time!

Choose whether the native speaker said the fifth word as 우 or 으.

Ex1.   ○ ○ ○ ○ ●

🔊   우 으 우 우 으   ⓐ 우   ⓑ 으 ✓

Q1. ○ ○ ○ ○ ●   Q2. ○ ○ ○ ○ ●

        ⓐ 우   ⓑ 으   ⓐ 우   ⓑ 으

Q3. ○ ○ ○ ○ ●   Q4. ○ ○ ○ ○ ●

        ⓐ 우   ⓑ 으   ⓐ 우   ⓑ 으

▶ Listen to the audio and choose the word that was said twice.

Ex2. 🔊 ○ ● ●
구 그 그

ⓐ 구 ✓ⓑ 그

Q5. ⓐ 굴 ⓑ 글   Q6. ⓐ 운 ⓑ 은   Q7. ⓐ 구만 ⓑ 그만

▶ Listen to the words and guess which vowels go in the blanks. After answering all the questions, listen again and read along.

Ex3.

구	름

✓ⓐ ㅜ, ㅡ ⓑ ㅡ, ㅜ

Q8.

ㄱ	룻

ⓐ ㅜ, ㅜ ⓑ ㅡ, ㅡ

Q9.

ㄴ	믈

ⓐ ㅜ, ㅜ ⓑ ㅡ, ㅡ

Q10.

ⓐ ㅜ, ㅡ ⓑ ㅡ, ㅜ

Q11.

ⓐ ㅜ, ㅡ ⓑ ㅡ, ㅜ

Q12.

ⓐ ㅜ, ㅡ ⓑ ㅡ, ㅜ

Let's practice with sentences!

▶ This time, let's practice ㅜ and ㅡ with sentences. Please read the sentences below slowly. Then practice reading them again faster and faster.

Q13. 현우 씨랑 경은 씨는 무릎이 안 좋아요.

↳ [혀누 씨랑 경은 씨는 무르피 안 조:아요.]

= Hyunwoo and Kyeong-eun have bad knees.

Q14. 근데, 은주 씨는 참 운이 좋네요.

↳ [근데, 은주 씨는 참 우:니 존:네요.]

= By the way, Eunjoo has very good luck.

Q15. 승무원 스무 명이 일을 그만둘 거예요.

↳ [승무원 스무 명이 이:를 그만둘 꺼예요.]

= Twenty flight attendants will quit.

Q16. 구 분 동안 문을 두드리세요.

↳ [구 분 똥안 무늘 두드리세요.]

= Knock on the door for nine minutes.

Q17. 제가 쓴 글 읽지 마세요. 부끄러워요.

↳ [제가 쓴 글 익찌 마:세요. 부끄러워요.]

= Don't read what I wrote. It's embarrassing.

Answers

Q1. ⓐ (으으으으우)

Q2. ⓑ (우으으으으)

Q3. ⓑ (으우우으으)

Q4. ⓐ (우으우으우)

Q5. ⓐ (굴굴글)

Q6. ⓑ (은운은)

Q7. ⓐ (구만-그만-구만)

Q8. ⓑ 그릇 (= bowl; dish)

Q9. ⓐ 눈물 (= tear)

Q10. ⓐ 아무튼 (= anyway)

Q11. ⓑ 승무원 (= flight attendant)

Q12. ⓐ 두드리세요 (= Knock/Beat at it.)

Real Experiences by Korean Learners

This anecdote shared by Matthew Enriquez, Australia

I was at a 맛집 having a small play fight with a friend when another friend said, "야~ 싸우지 마~".
So I thought, "Oh, the word for stop is 멈추다, right?" and said out loud, "몸 주다?" Both friends
stopped and looked at me blankly, like "뭐라고??" I asked, "멈추다 (pronounced as 몸 주다) is 'stop'
right?" They started laughing and said, "No, no, no. That sounds like 'give me your body'!"
Oops! ㅋㅋㅋㅋ큐ㅠㅠ

How To Sound Like A Native Korean Speaker

CHAPTER 3

How on Earth Should I Pronounce 의?

● How do you pronounce ─|? Have you ever tried pronouncing the vowel ─ followed quickly by the vowel |? Try reading the word below.

Were you able to pronounce 늬 well?

It is difficult, right?

Well, there is some good news.
When pronouncing 늬, you actually do not need to pronounce both the ─ and | vowels. You only need to pronounce the |.

(▶) Listen to the native speaker's pronunciation of "무늬 (pattern)".
01

The pronunciation of ─| varies depending on whether it stands alone, is combined with a consonant, or is at the beginning or end of a word. In this lesson we will learn how its pronunciation changes and practice it together.

1. When 의 is the first syllable of a word

● Please read the Korean words below.

의사 doctor   의자 chair

They are common words, right? In these two words, 의 is at the beginning of the word. In this case, 의 is pronounced as it looks, ─ + |.

의사   의자
[의사]   [의자]

2. When 의 is not the first syllable of a word

● **Now look at the word below.**

거의 almost

This time, 의 is the second syllable of the word. In this case, it is fine to
pronounce 의 as ㅡ + ㅣ, but native speakers often pronounce only the ㅣ
vowel for convenience. In other words, this word is often pronounced [거이].

▶ **Listen to the native speaker's pronunciation.**
03

거의
[거의] [거이]

3. Consonants + ㅢ

The vowel ㅢ found in "무늬 (pattern)" that we read aloud at the beginning of
this lesson was pronounced as ㅣ, right? 무늬 is not pronounced as [무늬],
but as [무니]. This is because when the ㅢ vowel combines with a consonant
and becomes a syllable, it is difficult to pronounce the ㅢ vowel as ㅡ + ㅣ.

무늬
[무니]

So then, how is the word below pronounced?

희망 hope, wish

That's right. It is pronounced as [히망].

(▶) **Listen and repeat.**
04

How is the word below pronounced?

문의 inquiry

According to what we learned above, since 의 is in the second syllable, can we pronounce this word as both [문:의] or [문:이]?

No. Since the final ㄴ in 문 moves to the first sound of the next syllable starting with a vowel, it becomes [무:늬]. When the ㅢ vowel is combined with a consonant to form a syllable, it is difficult to pronounce it as ㅡ + ㅣ, so it then becomes [무:니].

(▶) **Listen and repeat.**
05

문의 → [무:늬] → [무:니]

In the end, the two words, "무늬 (pattern)" and "문의 (inquiry)", are pronounced the same.

무늬 [무니] pattern

문의 [무:니] inquiry

Of course, 문의, which means inquiry, can also technically be pronounced as [무늬], and differs from "무늬 (pattern)" in that the first syllable is a long sound. But the two words are actually often pronounced the same in everyday conversation, so you have to distinguish the meaning based on context.

4. Postposition 의

Finally, when 의 is a postposition it indicates that the following noun is attached to or belongs to the noun preceding it.

● **Please read these expressions aloud.**

나의 가족 my family

저의 인생 my life

우리의 여행 our trip

This 의 can also be pronounced as ㅡ + ㅣ, but since it is not easy to say, many native speakers pronounce it as [에].

(▶) **Listen and repeat.**

06 나의 가족

[나의 가족] [나에 가족]

07 저의 인생

[저의 인생] [저에 인생]

08 우리의 여행

[우리의 여행] [우리에 여행]

Let's practice!

(▶) **Great! Now let's practice with some different words. First, we have some**
09 **words in which ㅢ can be pronounced as ㅣ. Listen and repeat.**

회의 [회:이] meeting; conference

예의 [예이] manners; etiquette

강의 [강:이] lecture

상의 [상이] discussion

주의 [주:이] caution, attention, warning

저희 [저히] we, our

How To Sound Like A Native Korean Speaker

흰색 [힌색] white color

편의점 [펴니점] convenience store

탈의실 [타리실] fitting room, locker room

Now let's look at words where ㅢ can be pronounced as ㅔ.

▶ **Listen and repeat.**
10

단어의 뜻 [단어에 뜯] the meaning of a word

최고의 선물 [최:고에 선:물] the best gift

하루의 대부분 [하루에 대:부분] most of the day

친구 중의 한 명 [친구 중에 한 명] one of my friends

그 사람의 말 [그 사:라메 말:] that person's words

최악의 실수 [최:아게 실쑤] the worst mistake

Quiz Time!

▶ Find and mark the correct pronunciation of the following words.

Q1. **의사소통** (= communication)

ⓐ [의:사소통]   ⓑ [이:사소통]

Q2. **강의실** (= lecture room, classroom)

    ⓐ [강:이실]   ⓑ [강:으실]

Q3. **희생** (= sacrifice)

    ⓐ [희생]   ⓑ [히생]

Q4. **띄어쓰기** (= word spacing)

    ⓐ [띄어쓰기]   ⓑ [띠어쓰기]

Q5. **말의 의미** (= the meaning of a word)

    ⓐ [마:레 이:미]   ⓑ [마:리 의:미]   ⓒ [마:레 의:미]

● **Once you have checked the correct answers, listen to the native speaker's pronunciation and read along. [Q1~5]**

▶ Lastly, let's practice ⁻ㅣ using sentences. First, read the sentence below slowly and then listen to the native speaker's pronunciation. Practice and repeat.

Q6. **강의실** 가기 전에 **편의점** 좀 들르자.

    = Let's stop by the convenience store before going to the classroom.

Q7. **의사** 선생님께서 **희망**이 **거의** 없다고 하셨어요.

    = The doctor said that there is very little hope.

Q8. 그 사람 **말의 의미**를 모르겠어요.

= I don't know what that person is trying to say.

Q9. 예의 없이 행동하다가 **주의**를 받았어요.

= I got a warning while acting rudely.

Q10. 눈알의 흰 부분을 **흰자**라고 해요.

= The white part of the eye is called the sclera.

Answers

Q1. ⓐ   Q2. ⓐ   Q3. ⓑ   Q4. ⓑ   Q5. ⓒ

CHAPTER 4.

Transformers

Lesson 1 - 1

Doubles in Disguise

● **Read the two words below aloud.**

신사 gentleman 식사 meal

▶ **Listen to the native speaker's pronunciation.**
01

What do you think? The 사 in 신사 and the 사 in 식사 sound different, right?

신사 is pronounced just as it looks, but 식사 is pronounced [식싸]. Why might this be?

신사 [신ː사]

식사 [식싸]

The reason is that when ㄱ, ㄷ, ㅂ, ㅅ, or ㅈ come after the final consonant sounds [ㄱ], [ㄷ], or [ㅂ], they are pronounced as [ㄲ], [ㄸ], [ㅃ], [ㅆ], and [ㅉ].

● **Let's look at some words that are like this.**

식당 [식땅] restaurant

습관 [습꽌] habit

혹시 [혹씨] by any chance

늦잠 [늗짬] oversleeping; rising late

낮잠 [낟짬] nap

▶ **Listen to the native speaker and repeat.**
02

● **Let's practice with a sentence this time.**

이 산은 생각보다 높고 험해요.

= This mountain is higher and harder than you think.

How do you pronounce 생각보다 in the sentence above? That's right. It is pronounced like [생각뽀다]. What about 높고? Yes. You pronounce it as [놉꼬].

이 산은 생각보다 높고 험해요.

▶ **Listen to the native speaker and repeat.**
03

[이 사는 생각뽀다 놉꼬 험:해요.]

Even in some instances where there is a space between the final sounds [ㄱ], [ㄷ], or [ㅂ] and the following syllable that starts with ㄱ, ㄷ, ㅂ, ㅅ, or ㅈ, if you say the two words in one breath without a pause, ㄱ, ㄷ, ㅂ, ㅅ, and ㅈ are pronounced [ㄲ], [ㄸ], [ㅃ], [ㅆ], and [ㅉ].

어제 삼십 분밖에 못 잤어요.

= Yesterday I could only sleep for 30 minutes.

Here, because it is almost always pronounced as one word, 삼십 분 is pronounced as [삼십뿐]. Similarly, because 못 잤어요 is pronounced like it is one word more often than not, it is pronounced as [몯:짜써요].

어제 삼십 분밖에 못 잤어요.

▶ **Listen to the native speaker and repeat.**

04

[어제 삼십뿐바께 몯:짜써요.]

Pop Quiz!

● In the words below, if the underlined syllable's first sound is pronounced as [ㄲ], [ㄸ], [ㅃ], [ㅆ], or [ㅉ], mark it with a check mark.

1. 약속 promise; plan ( )

2. 연습 practice ( )

3. 답장 reply ( )

4. 신발 shoes ( )

5. 학교 school ( )

6. 학생 student (   )

7. 감기 cold; flu (   )

8. 집중 concentration (   )

9. 듣기 listening (   )

10. 말하기 speaking (   )

When the final consonant sounds [ㄱ], [ㄷ], or [ㅂ] are followed by ㄱ, ㄷ, ㅂ, ㅅ, or ㅈ, the pronunciation becomes [ㄲ], [ㄸ], [ㅃ], [ㅆ], and [ㅉ]. Therefore the correct answers are 1, 3, 5, 6, 8, and 9!

Listen to the native speaker's pronunciation of the 10 words and follow along.

Q1

Lesson 1 - 2

Decepti-consonants

● **Read the word below aloud.**

신고 report; declaration

▶ **Check the native speaker's pronunciation.**
05

● **This time, try pronouncing the word 신고, which combines the word 신다, which means "to wear (shoes/socks)", with the suffix –고, which means "and".**

신고 (one) wears (shoes/socks) and...

▶ **Check the native speaker's pronunciation.**
06

신고 [신고] declaration

신고 [신ː꼬] (one) wears (shoes/socks) and...

These two words are both spelled 신고, but the way they are pronounced is very different, isn't it?

As is the case for the second 신고, when the stem of a verb or adjective is combined with a suffix beginning in ㄱ, ㄷ, ㅅ, or ㅈ, and the stem's final consonant is [ㄴ] or [ㅁ], then the first consonant of the suffix is pronounced as [ㄲ], [ㄸ], [ㅆ], or [ㅉ].

▶ **Take a look at the examples below.**

안(다) + -고 = 안고 [안:꼬]
to hug   and   (one) hugs (someone) and...

머리를 감(다) + -기 전에
to wash one's hair   before

= 머리를 감기 전에 [머리를 감:끼 저네]
     before washing one's hair

숨(다) + -다가 = 숨다가 [숨:따가]
to hide   while   while hiding

참(다) + -지 마세요
to hold back   Don't...

= 참지 마세요 [참:찌 마:세요]
     Don't hold back.

▶ This time, let's practice with sentences.

08 **동생이 제 신발을 신고 나갔어요.**
↳ [동생이 제 신바를 신:꼬 나가써요.]
= My younger sibling went out wearing my shoes.

09 **엄마가 저를 안고 사랑한다고 말했어요.**
↳ [엄마가 저를 안:꼬 사랑한다고 말:해써요.]
= My mother held me in her arms and told me she loves me.

10 **머리를 감기 전에 이부터 닦으세요.**
↳ [머리를 감:끼 저네 이부터 다끄세요.]
= Before washing your hair, brush your teeth first.

11 **안 보이게 숨다가 들켰어요.**
↳ [안 보이게 숨:따가 들켜써요.]
= I was hiding so I wouldn't be seen, but then I got caught.

12 **화장실 가고 싶으면 이야기하세요. 참지 마세요.**
↳ [화장실 가고 시프면 이야기하세요. 참:찌 마:세요.]
= Let me know if you want to go to the restroom. Don't hold it in.

● **Check the native speaker's pronunciation.**

● **What do you think? Did you pronounce everything correctly? Try reading along while listening one more time.**

Pop Quiz!

● If the pronunciation of the underlined part in both sentence A and sentence B are the same, mark it as O. If they are different, mark it as X.

1. ( )

A. 신발 <u>**신기**</u> 전에 이것 좀 보세요.

= Take a look at this before you put on your shoes.

B. 우와, <u>**신기**</u>해요!

= Wow, that's interesting!

2. ( )

A. 여기서 머리 <u>**감기**</u> 불편해요.

= It is inconvenient to wash my hair here.

B. <u>**감기**</u> 걸렸어요?

= Did you catch a cold?

3. ( )

A. <u>**참고**</u> 기다리세요.

= Please be patient and wait.

B. 이 자료 <u>**참고**</u>하세요.

= Please refer to this material.

How did you do? All three questions should be marked X.

The underlined parts of the A sentences are all combinations of stems that end in ㄴ or ㅁ and suffixes that begin in ㄱ, so the first ㄱ sound of the suffixes are all pronounced as [ㄲ]. On the other hand, the underlined part of the B sentences are all single words, so the ㄱ is pronounced as is.

Listen to the native speaker's pronunciation and follow along.

1'.

A. 신발 **신기** 전에 이것 좀 보세요.

↳ [신발 신:끼 저네 이걷쫌 보세요.]

B. 우와, **신기**해요!

↳ [우와, 신기해요!]

2'.

A. 여기서 머리 **감기** 불편해요.

↳ [여기서 머리 감:끼 불편해요.]

B. **감기** 걸렸어요?

↳ [감기 걸려써요?]

3'.

A. **참고** 기다리세요.

↳ [참:꼬 기다리세요.]

B. 이 자료 **참고**하세요.

↳ [이 자료 참고하세요.]

Lesson 1 - 3

Space Bridge

● **Read the word below aloud.**

먹을 거 something to eat

How did you pronounce it?

(▶) **Check the native speaker's pronunciation.**

13

That's right. It is not pronounced [머글거], but rather [머글꺼].

In 먹을 거, the -(으)ㄹ is a connective ending that is needed to change a verb in the future tense into an adjective. If ㄱ, ㄷ, ㅂ, ㅅ, or ㅈ come after this connective ending, they are pronounced as [ㄲ], [ㄸ], [ㅃ], [ㅆ], or [ㅉ].

-(으)ㄹ + ㄱ, ㄷ, ㅂ, ㅅ, ㅈ ➡ -(으)ㄹ [ㄲ], [ㄸ], [ㅃ], [ㅆ], [ㅉ]

● **Read the expressions below out loud.**

할 거 something to do

쓸 거 something to write with; something to use

볼 거 something to watch

마실 거 something to drink

갈 데 a place to go

살 데 a place to buy (something)

놀 데 a place to hang out

(▶) **Check the native speaker's pronunciation.**
14

That's right. These expressions are all pronounced in this manner as well: [할꺼],
[쓸꺼], [볼꺼], [마실꺼], [갈떼], [살떼], and [놀:떼].

(▶) **Shall we practice with sentences?**

15 **부산에 갈 데 많죠.**
   ↳ [부사네 갈떼 만:초.]
   = Of course, there are a lot of places to go/visit in Busan.

16 **여기 놀 데 별로 없어요.**
   ↳ [여기 놀:떼 별로 업:써요.]
   = There are not many places to hang out here.

17 **마실 거 좀 줄까요?**
   ↳ [마실꺼 좀 줄까요?]
   = Do you want something to drink?

18 **할 거 없으면 저 좀 도와주세요.**
   ↳ [할꺼 업:쓰면 저 좀 도와주세요.]
   = If you don't have anything to do, please help me.

19 주변에 살 데가 없어요.

↳ [주벼네 살떼가 업:써요.]

= There is nowhere to buy (it) around me.

20 요즘 영화관에 볼 거 없어요.

↳ [요즘 영화과네 볼꺼 업:써요.]

= There is nothing to watch at the movie theater these days.

Did you read them all?

● **This time, listen and repeat.**

Even among the suffixes we know, there are many instances in which the modifying suffix -(으)ㄹ is used.

● **Let's take a look at some examples.**

-(으)ㄹ 거예요 will

-(으)ㄹ 수 있어요 can

-(으)ㄹ 줄 알아요 can; know how to...

-(으)ㄹ 것 같아요 I think one will...

-(으)ㄹ게요 I will

-(으)ㄹ수록 the more... the more...

● **Read the six suffixes above out loud.**

▶ **Listen to the native speaker's pronunciation.**

21

How To Sound Like A Native Korean Speaker

As you heard, the consonants following -(으)ㄹ are all pronounced as their more tensed double consonant forms.

▶ This time, shall we practice with some sentences? Read the sentences below out loud.

22 누가 끌 거예요?

↳ [누가 끌:꺼예요?]

= Who will turn it off?

23 이거 그릴 수 있어요?

↳ [이거 그:릴쑤 이써요?]

= Can you draw this?

24 피아노 칠 줄 알아요?

↳ [피아노 칠쭈라라요?]

= Do you know how to play the piano?

25 금방 지칠 것 같아요.

↳ [금방 지:칠껃 가타요.]

= I think I will get tired of it very soon.

26 제가 잠글게요.

↳ [제가 잠글께요.]

= Let me lock it up.

27 영화는 길수록 좋아요.

↳ [영화는 길:쑤록 조:아요.]

= The longer the movie is, the more I like it.

● **Listen to the native speaker's pronunciation and follow along.**

More Than Meets the Eye

● **Read the three words below aloud.**

출발 departure, leave

출동 move out; mobilize

출구 exit

▶ **Listen to the native speaker's pronunciation.**

28

That's right. They are each pronounced like this, right?

[출발] [출똥] [출구]

These three words all have three things in common.

- All three words are hanja based: 출발(出發), 출동(出動), and 출구(出口).
- All three words are comprised of two syllables.
- The first syllable of each word is 출.

However, when pronounced, only in the second word, 출동, does the ㄷ change to [ㄸ]. 출발 and 출구 are not pronounced as [출빨] or [출꾸]. Why is that?

This is because in two-syllable hanja-based words in which the first syllable ends in ㄹ, and the second syllable begins with ㄷ, ㅅ, or ㅈ, the first sound of the second syllable is pronounced as [ㄸ], [ㅆ], or [ㅉ].

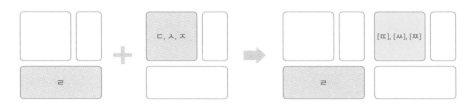

What are some other words like this?

Listen and read along.

29

실수(失手) [실쑤] mistake

결정(決定) [결쩡] decision

결석(缺席) [결썩] absence

발전(發展) [발쩐] development; advancement

열정(熱情) [열쩡] passion

일정(日程) [일쩡] program; schedule; itinerary

결제(決濟) [결쩨] payment; settlement

활동(活動) [활똥] activity; movement; campaign

갈등(葛藤) [갈뜽] conflict

결심(決心) [결씸] resolution; determination

- This rule applies to words other than nouns, too.

일단(一旦) [일딴] first, for now, once

절대(絶對) [절때] absolutely; never

Have you practiced enough?

- **Let's practice with sentences this time. First, read them aloud.**

일단 제가 먼저 결제할게요.

= Anyway, I will pay first for now.

실수할 것 같아요.

= I think I will make a mistake.

활동하다가 갈등이 생겼어요.

= Conflicts arose while (we were) touring.

* Celebrities usually use the word 활동
하다 instead of the word 일하다 when
talking about what they do, including
appearing on TV, filming, touring,
promoting, etc.

결석은 절대 안 돼요.

= Absences will not be tolerated.

현우 씨는 일단 결심하면 열정적으로 할 거예요.

= As for Hyunwoo, once he makes up his mind, he will do it passionately.

▶ This time, listen to the native speaker and follow along. While listening, check not only their pronunciation, but also their intonation and the places where they take a breath.

30 **일단 제가 먼저 결제할게요.**

↳ [일딴 제가 먼저 결쩨할께요.]

31 실수할 것 같아요.

↳ [실쑤할껀 가타요.]

32 활동하다가 갈등이 생겼어요.

↳ [활똥하다가 갈뜽이 생겨써요.]

33 결석은 절대 안 돼요.

↳ [결써근 절때 안 돼요.]

34 현우 씨는 일단 결심하면 열정적으로 할 거예요.

↳ [혀누 씨는 일딴 결씸하면 열쩡저그로 할꺼예요.]

Pop Quiz!

● If the pronunciation of the underlined part in both word ⓐ and word ⓑ are the same, mark it as O. If they are different, mark it as X.

1. (   )   ⓐ **등** back   ⓑ **갈등** conflict

2. (   )   ⓐ **결심** resolution; determination   ⓑ **심장** heart

3. (   )   ⓐ **결과** result   ⓑ **과일** fruit

4. (   )   ⓐ **활동** activity; movement; campaign   ⓑ **동전** coin

5. (   )   ⓐ **실수** mistake   ⓑ **할 수 있어요.** I can do it.

6. (   )   ⓐ **결정** decision   ⓑ **일정** program; schedule; itinerary

Answers

1. X 2. X 3. ○ 4. X 5. ○ 6. ○

In the cases of 등, 심장, 결과, 과일, and 동전, the underlined parts are pronounced as they are written.

Whoa! What a long journey! You've done a great job getting this far. Bravo!

There are so many cases where certain consonants are pronounced as double consonants, right?

It would be nearly impossible to tell at first glance which words and phrases follow these rules and exceptions just by trying to memorize them all.
As is often the case, there are many exceptions to the rules. Rather than memorizing each word and every rule, it is would be much faster to find out the pronunciation of a word by looking it up in the dictionary.

That being said, knowing that these kinds of rules exist and practicing the pronunciation of words that fall under these rules is very helpful. When you come across a new word in the future, even if you don't check the pronunciation from a native speaker, you will find yourself automatically pronouncing the words correctly all on your own.

Lesson 2 - 1

Throw Away the Rules!

● **Read the two words below out loud.**

잠자리 dragonfly   잠자리 bed

▶ **Listen to the native speaker's pronunciation.**

01

What do you think? They are spelled exactly the same way but pronounced differently, right?

The word meaning dragonfly, 잠자리, is pronounced [잠자리], while the word for the place in which you sleep, 잠자리, is pronounced [잠짜리]. Why might this be?

잠자리 [잠자리] dragonfly

잠자리 [잠짜리] bed

Although they are spelled the same, there is a difference between the two words. The second 잠자리 is actually a combination of two separate words.

잠자리 = 잠 sleep + 자리 place; space

There is another word very similar to this one.

일자리 job, work

This word is also a combination word.

일 work + 자리 place; space ⋯▸ 일자리 job

So, how should this word be pronounced?

That's right. 일자리 is just like 잠자리 in that the 자리 is pronounced as [짜리].

일자리 [일:짜리]

▶ **Listen to the native speaker's pronunciation and repeat.**
02

잠자리 and 일자리 do not follow any of the four rules you learned in Lesson 1, so why is 자 pronounced as [짜]? That is precisely why the title of this lesson is, "Throw Away the Rules!"

Regardless of the rules, there are words that are always pronounced in their hard consonant form whenever they come after other nouns. 자리 is one of these words.

● **Shall we look at some other words that are like this as well?**

"집 (house)" on its own refers to a place where people or animals live, but when attached to the end of another noun, it also means "shop". So 빵집 refers to a shop that sells bread, not where bread lives, and 피자집 refers to a shop that sells pizza, not where pizza lives. In these cases, 집 is pronounced as [찝], not [집], regardless of the word that precedes it.

빵집 [빵찝] bakery ◀··· 빵 bread + 집 store

피자집 [피자찝] pizza place ◀··· 피자 pizza + 집 store

The same goes for 값, which means "price". When written after another noun, 값 is pronounced as [깝], not [갑].

빵값 [빵깝] price of bread ◀··· 빵 bread + 값 price

커피값 [커피깝] price of coffee ◀··· 커피 coffee + 값 price

집값 [집깝] house price ◀··· 집 house + 값 price

Speaking of food, 밥 is also frequently pronounced as [빱] when it comes after a noun.

아침밥 [아침빱] breakfast ◀··· 아침 morning; breakfast + 밥 meal; rice

점심밥 [점:심빱] lunch ◀··· 점심 lunch + 밥 meal; rice

저녁밥 [저녁빱] dinner ◀··· 저녁 evening; dinner + 밥 meal; rice

Actually, it is enough to just say 아침, 점심, and 저녁 without adding 밥, but 아침, 점심, and 저녁 also have the meaning of "morning", "lunchtime", and "evening", so people often attach 밥 to these words in order to clearly refer to meals.

The same is true of 김밥 and 비빔밥, dishes that you all know.

▶ **Listen to the native speaker's pronunciation and follow along.**

06

김밥 [김:빱] gimbap ◀••• 김 dried seaweed ＋ 밥 rice

비빔밥 [비빔빱] bibimbap ◀••• 비빔 mixing ＋ 밥 rice

* gimbap: seaweed rice rolls

* bibimbap: rice mixed with meat and assorted vegetables

"Gimbap" is sometimes pronounced as [김:밥], but most people pronounce it as [김:빱].

When the word 병 is added after another noun, it is also pronounced as [뼝]. The word 병 has two meanings: "bottle" and "disease". If either are placed after a noun, they are pronounced in their hard consonant form.

▶ **Listen to the native speaker's pronunciation and follow along.**

07

물병 [물뼝] water bottle ◀••• 물 water ＋ 병 bottle

콜라병 [콜라뼝] Coke bottle ◀••• 콜라 Coke ＋ 병 bottle

눈병 [눈뼝] eye infection ◀••• 눈 eye ＋ 병 disease

피부병 [피부뼝] skin disease ◀••• 피부 skin ＋ 병 disease

That is why 공주병 and 왕자병, the slang words referring to someone who sees themselves as a "princess" or "prince" and acts as such, are pronounced like [공주뼝] and [왕자뼝]!

So far, we have looked at compound words that are combinations of two nouns that can also be used alone. This time, let's look at some cases where the beginning consonant of the suffix is pronounced in its hard consonant form. In these examples a suffix is added to a noun that can also stand alone.

● **The first is a suffix we use very often, −권. −권 means "ticket".**

▶ 항공권 [항:공꿘] plane ticket ◀··· 항공 flight ＋ -권 ticket
08
입장권 [입짱꿘] entrance ticket ◀··· 입장 admission ＋ -권 ticket

You may have also often seen -법, a suffix that means "method" or "rule".
● **The suffix −법 is also often pronounced in its stressed double consonant form.**

▶ 사용법 [사:용뻡] instructions ◀··· 사용 use ＋ -법 method
09
맞춤법 [맏춤뻡] spelling rule ◀··· 맞춤 assembling ＋ -법 method

● **The word for law, 법, is not a suffix, but as expected, when it is written after a noun, it is also pronounced as [뻡].**

▶ 기본법 [기본뻡] fundamental law ◀··· 기본 basics ＋ 법 law
10
복지법 [복찌뻡] welfare law ◀··· 복지 welfare ＋ 법 law

Shall we practice with some sentences now?

● Read the sentences slowly, putting each word in the blank one by one. Then, practice along with the native speaker's pronunciation, intonation, and speed.

▶ **11**

_____ 먹었어요?

= Did you have _____?

· 아침밥   · 점심밥   · 저녁밥

▶ **12**

이 앞에 _____ 생겼어요.

= There is a new _____ across the street.

· 빵집   · 피자집   · 김밥집   · 비빔밥집

▶ **13**

_____ 누가 냈어요?

= Who paid for _____?

· 빵값   · 커피값

▶ **14**

_____이 너무 비싸요.

= _____ is too expensive.

· 집값   · 항공권   · 입장권

15 이 _____ 모양이 너무 예뻐요.

= The shape of this _____ is so pretty.

· 물병   · 콜라병

16 _____ 잘 알아요?

= Do you know _____ well?

· 사용법   · 맞춤법

17 저희 집 강아지가 _____에 걸렸어요.

= My puppy got _____.

· 눈병   · 피부병

Lesson 2 - 2

Just Memorize It!

Lastly, we are going to take a look at a few cases where consonants are pronounced in their double consonant form... for absolutely no obvious reason. There are no rules or patterns, so all we can do is memorize them. If you practice saying them many times, you will wind up memorizing them automatically without any extra effort.

● **First, read the following words aloud.**

인기	열쇠	문자	성격
popularity	key; clue	letter; text message	personality; character

조건	사건	경찰서	물고기
condition	incident	police station	fish

▶ **Now, listen to the native speaker's pronunciation. While listening, mark the**
18 **words you pronounced incorrectly with a check mark.**

인기 [인끼]   (   )

열쇠 [열ː쐬]   (   )

문자 [문짜]   (   )

성격 [성:껵]   (   )

조건 [조껀]   (   )

사건 [사:껀]   (   )

경찰서 [경:찰써]   (   )

물고기 [물꼬기]   (   )

Shall we practice now with some sentences?

● **First, read them aloud.**

석진 씨는 **성격**이 좋아서 **인기**가 많아요.

= Seokjin has a good personality, so he is very popular.

경찰서에서 **사건**을 조사 중이에요.

= They are investigating the incident at the police station.

문자로 **물고기** 이모티콘을 보냈어요.

= I texted him/her the fish emoticon.

열쇠를 주는 대신에 **조건**이 있어요.

= In return for giving you the key, there is a condition.

▶ 19 Now, listen to the native speaker's pronunciation. As before, mark the sentences you pronounced incorrectly with a check mark.

석진 씨는 **성격이** 좋아서 **인기가** 많아요. (   )
↳ [석찐 씨는 성:껴기 조:아서 인끼가 마:나요.]

경찰서에서 **사건을** 조사 중이에요. (   )
↳ [경:찰써에서 사:꺼늘 조사 중이에요.]

문자로 물고기 이모티콘을 보냈어요. (   )
↳ [문짜로 물꼬기 이모티콘을 보내써요.]

열쇠를 주는 대신에 **조건이** 있어요. (   )
↳ [열:쐬를 주는 대:시네 조꺼니 이써요.]

Pop Quiz!

Wait! Before taking the quiz, read the words and sentences that you marked with a check above out loud while looking at the phonetic transcriptions one more time.

Good. Shall we take the quiz now?

- Take a look at the following pairs of words. Place a check mark next to the word where the first sound of the underlined syllable is pronounced as [ㄲ], [ㄸ], [ㅃ], [ㅆ], or [ㅉ].

1. 인기 (   )   **연기** (   )
popularity   acting; delay; smoke

2. **불고기** (　　　)　　　**물고기** (　　　)
　　bulgogi　　　　　　　　fish

3. **문자** (　　　)　　　**기자** (　　　)
　　letter; text message　　reporter

4. **수건** (　　　)　　　**조건** (　　　)
　　towel　　　　　　　　condition

5. **성격** (　　　)　　　**자격** (　　　)
　　personality; character　qualification

This time, if the pronunciations of the underlined syllables are the same, mark it as O. If they are different, mark it as X.

6. **문자**　　　**가짜**　　　　☐ O　　☐ X
　　letter; text message　fake

7. **가격**　　　**성격**　　　　☐ O　　☐ X
　　price　　　personality; character

8. **조건**　　　**사건**　　　　☐ O　　☐ X
　　condition　incident

9. **열쇠**　　　**자물쇠**　　　☐ O　　☐ X
　　key　　　　lock

10. **경찰서**　　**소방서**　　　☐ O　　☐ X
　　police station　fire station

Answers

1. 인기 (인기 [인끼], 연기 [연기])

2. 물고기 (불고기 [불고기], 물고기 [물꼬기])

3. 문자 (문자 [문짜], 기자 [기자])

4. 조건 (수건 [수:건], 조건 [조껀])

5. 성격 (성격 [성:껵], 자격 [자격])

6. O (문자 [문짜], 가짜 [가:짜])

7. X (가격 [가격], 성격 [성:껵])

8. O (조건 [조껀], 사건 [사:껀])

9. O (열쇠 [열:쐬], 자물쇠 [자물쐬])

10. X (경찰서 [경:찰써], 소방서 [소방서])

▶ Once you have checked your answers, listen to the native speaker's
Q1 pronunciation and follow along.

How To Sound Like A Native Korean Speaker

Lesson 3

Follow My Lead!

- **Read the word below.**

기억 memory

- **Now read this word below.**

기억나요. I remember.

 Listen to the native speaker's pronunciation.

01

기억 [기억]

기억나요. [기엉나요.]

When only the word 기억 is pronounced, the final consonant ㄱ at the end of the word is pronounced as [ㄱ]. However, when the sentence 기억나요 is said, the final consonant ㄱ of the word 기억 is pronounced as an [ㅇ] sound.

This is the pronunciation phenomenon that we will introduce in this lesson. As in this example, when a non-nasal consonant meets a nasal ㄴ or ㅁ sound, it is changed into a nasalized sound itself.

- Read the sentence below.

생각났어요.

As in 기억나요 earlier, the final consonant [ㄱ] is in front of the nasal [ㄴ] sound in 생각났어요. Therefore in this case as well, the final consonant [ㄱ] is pronounced as [ㅇ].

▶ **Shall we practice?**

02

생각났어요. [생강나써요.] I remembered it.

Can you think of what the pronunciations of [ㄱ] and [ㅇ] might have in common?

- **Read the two words below, focusing on the pronunciation at the end of the last syllable.**

생각 [생각] thought, memory

생강 [생강] ginger

Did you feel it? Yes, [ㄱ] and [ㅇ] are said from the same place in your throat. There are three nasal sounds in Korean: [ㄴ], [ㅁ], and [ㅇ]. Now you probably understand why the final consonant sound [ㄱ] was changed to the [ㅇ] sound among the three nasal sounds, right?

- **This time, read the expression below aloud.**

듣는 중 in the middle of listening

▶ Now listen to the native speaker's pronunciation.

That is right. It is pronounced [듣는 중].

Since ㄴ is a nasal sound, the final consonant sound [ㄷ] is also changed to a nasal sound.

Just as the final consonant sound [ㄱ] is changed to [ㅇ], a nasal sound with a similar position of articulation in the throat, the final consonant sound [ㄷ] is pronounced as [ㄴ]. Among the nasal sounds [ㄴ], [ㅁ], and [ㅇ], [ㄴ] is pronounced from the same position in your throat that [ㄷ] is.

● **Listen to the native speaker's pronunciation of "듣는 중 [듣는 중]" again, and this time, try following along.**

Now, shall we look at an example where the final consonant [ㅂ] is pronounced as a nasalized sound when it comes before another nasal sound?

 appetite

▶ **Listen to the native speaker's pronunciation.**

Did you notice how the final consonant [ㅂ] was pronounced in front of the nasal sound [ㅁ]? Among the three nasal sounds, [ㄴ], [ㅁ], and [ㅇ], it was pronounced as [ㅁ], a sound that you also make with a closed mouth just like [ㅂ].

입맛 [임맏]

● Listen to the native speaker's pronunciation of "입맛 [임맏]" again, and this time, try following along.

Here is a brief summary of what we learned above.

		+	ㄴ, ㅁ		⇒			ㄴ, ㅁ	
[ㄱ], [ㄷ], [ㅂ]						[ㅇ], [ㄴ], [ㅁ]			

● Now, let's practice with several words containing nasal sounds by reading them out loud.

▶ 05

[ㄱ] → [ㅇ]

작년	[장년]	last year
한국말	[한ː궁말]	Korean language
박물관	[방물관]	museum
국내선	[궁내선]	domestic flight
목말라요.	[몽말라요.]	I am thirsty.
백만장자	[뱅만장자]	millionaire

[ㄷ] → [ㄴ]

06

옛날	[옌:날]	the old days, the old times, the past
그것만	[그건만]	that thing only
좋네요.	[존:네요.]	It is good.
재미있는 이야기	[재미인는 이야기]	interesting story
끝났어요?	[끈나써요?]	Is it over?
빛나요.	[빈나요.]	It shines.

[ㅂ] → [ㅁ]

07

감사합니다.	[감:사함니다.]	Thank you.
월급날	[월금날]	payday
십만	[심만]	hundred thousand
겁나요?	[검나요?]	Are you scared?
좀 춥네요.	[좀 춤네요.]	It is a little cold.

재미없는 이야기　　　[재미엄는 이야기]　　　boring story

What do you think? If the final consonant immediately before a nasal sound is not a nasal sound itself, doesn't it become much easier to pronounce when you change it to a nasal sound as well?

Therefore, the same phenomenon occurs not only when the final consonants [ㄱ], [ㄷ], or [ㅂ] and the initial consonants [ㄴ] or [ㅁ] meet in one word, but also when they meet when two words are pronounced like one word in a single breath.

● **Read the sentences below.**

밥 먹었어요? Have you eaten?

오늘 못 만나요. I can't meet you today.

몇 명이에요? How many people are you?

▶ **Listen to the native speaker's pronunciation this time.**

08

[밤머거써요?]

[오늘 몬:만나요.]

[면명이에요?]

It is pronounced like this, right?

Instead of saying [밤머거써요], try pronouncing it as [밥머거써요]. It is difficult, right? For it to work, you have to rest for a moment after saying [밥] before you pronounce [머거써요]. In the same way, if you pronounce [몬:만나요] as [몯:만나요], you have to pause for a moment after saying [몯:] before pronouncing [만나요] for it to work. Phrases like 밥 먹다, 못 만나다, and 몇 명 are used so often in everyday speech that they are pronounced as one word the majority of the time. Therefore, they are pronounced more naturally as [밤먹따], [몬:만나다], and [면명].

This phenomenon, where the final consonants [ㄱ], [ㄷ], and [ㅂ] are changed to a nasal consonant sound when followed by another nasal consonant sound, is a very powerful pronunciation phenomenon in Korean. Have you ever heard Korean speakers pronounce the English greeting "good morning" like "[gʊn mɔːrnɪŋ]"? This is because they are applying this same nasalization phenomenon to English. It is such a familiar pronunciation phenomenon for native Korean speakers that they naturally wind up applying it even when speaking other languages, so practice until it feels natural for you, too!

Quiz Time!

● Choose the correct pronunciation of the word.

Q1. 작년 last year

ⓐ [장년] ⓑ [잔년] ⓒ [잠년]

Q2. 좋네요. It is good.

ⓐ [종:네요] ⓑ [존:네요] ⓒ [좀:네요]

Q3. 십만 원 100,000 won

ⓐ [싱마뭔] ⓑ [신마뭔] ⓒ [심마뭔]

Q4. 거짓말 lie

ⓐ [거:징말] ⓑ [거:진말] ⓒ [거:짐말]

Q5. 국민 nation; people

ⓐ [궁민] ⓑ [군민] ⓒ [굼민]

If the pronunciation of the underlined parts of both A and B are the same, mark it with an O. If they are different, mark it with an X.

Q6. ( ) ⓐ **밥맛** appetite

ⓑ **밥** rice, meal

Q7. ( ) ⓐ **생각났어요.** I remembered it.

ⓑ **생강** ginger

Q8. ( ) ⓐ **국민** nation; people

ⓑ **국가대표** national team

Q9. ( ) ⓐ **콧물** runny nose

ⓑ **콧노래** humming

Q10. ( ) ⓐ **듣고 있어요.** I am listening.

ⓑ **듣는 중이에요.** I am in the middle of listening.

Q11. ( ) ⓐ **맞는 것을 고르세요.** Choose the correct one.

ⓑ **만두** dumpling

▶ **Listen to the words and expressions from the quiz and repeat.**
Q1~11

Let's practice with sentences!

▶ Pay attention to the parts in bold and read them slowly and accurately. Then, listen to the native speaker's pronunciation. Following the pronunciation, intonation, and speed of the native speaker, practice several times.

Q12. 생각났어요! 그거 한국말로 생강이에요.

= I remember! That's 생강 (ginger) in Korean.

Q13. 눈을 보니까 거짓말 맞네요.

= Looking at your eyes, I can tell that is a lie.

Q14. 월급날이 되면 콧노래가 나와요.

= When payday comes, I hum.

Q15. 나 지금 밥 먹는 중이야.

= I'm eating right now.

Q16. 오늘 모임에 못 나오는 사람 몇 명이에요?

= How many people are unable to come to the gathering today?

Answers

Q1. ⓐ	Q5. ⓐ	Q9. O (ⓐ [콘물] ⓑ [콘노래])
Q2. ⓑ	Q6. X (ⓐ 밥맛 [밤맏] ⓑ [밥])	Q10. X (ⓐ [듣꼬 이써요] ⓑ [든는 중이에요])
Q3. ⓒ	Q7. O (ⓐ [생강나써요] ⓑ [생강])	Q11. O (ⓐ [만는 거슬 고르세요] ⓑ [만두])
Q4. ⓑ	Q8. X (ⓐ [궁민] ⓑ [국까대표]	

Lesson 4

When in Rome...

How would you pronounce 류 in the words below?

종류 kind; sort, category, type   **석류** pomegranate

ⓐ [류] ⓑ [뉴] ⓒ [유]

▶ **How would a native speaker pronounce it? Take a listen.**
01

The native speaker pronounced the 류 in both words as [뉴]. In addition, the final consonant in the first syllable of 석류 was pronounced as [ㅇ].

종류 [종ː뉴] kind; sort, category, type

석류 [성뉴] pomegranate

In the previous lesson, we practiced examples in which the final consonants [ㄱ], [ㄷ], and [ㅂ] came before a nasalized sound and so were changed to nasalized sounds themselves.

In this lesson, we will practice examples in which ㄹ comes after the final consonants [ㅁ], [ㅇ], [ㄱ], or [ㅂ] and is therefore pronounced as the nasalized [ㄴ].

First, let's take a look at some examples similar to the word we read above, "종류 [종ː뉴]", where ㄹ comes after the nasal final consonants [ㅁ] or [ㅇ].

음료수 [음:뇨수] drink, beverage

정류장 [정뉴장] stop, station

능력 [능녁] ability; capability

동료 [동뇨] coworker, colleague

대통령 [대:통녕] president

등록금 [등녹끔] tuition

장르 [장느] genre

심리학 [심니학] psychology

입장료 [입짱뇨] admission, entrance fee

Now let's try practicing some slightly harder words. There are some words in Korean that are formed by combining a noun with the affix −력. The affix −력 means "ability" or "power". Some nouns that are combined with −력 have the final sound [ㅇ]. When pronouncing these words, −력 should be pronounced as [녁].

▶ Let's practice together.
03

영향력 [영:향녁] influence

상상력 [상:상녁] imagination

적응력 [저긍녁] adaptability

경쟁력 [경ː쟁녁] competitiveness

가창력 [가창녁] singing ability

Among the affixes that start with ㄹ, there is an affix that adds the meaning of "ratio": -률. If the last sound of the word in front of -률 is a nasal sound, then -률 is pronounced as [뉼].

Shall we practice?

경쟁률 [경ː쟁뉼] competition rate

시청률 [시ː청뉼] television ratings

출생률 [출쌩뉼] birth rate

This time, we will look at examples where the ㄹ that comes after the final consonants [ㄱ] or [ㅂ] is pronounced as the nasalized [ㄴ]. In this case, it is not only the ㄹ that changes to a nasal sound, but the final consonants [ㄱ] and [ㅂ] are also changed to nasalized sounds.

First, let's look at when the final consonant sound [ㄱ] meets the initial consonant ㄹ.

Earlier, we learned that 석류 should be pronounced as [성뉴].

석류 [성뉴] pomegranate

Then, how should the word 국립, which means "national", as in "national museum" and "national university", be pronounced?

● **Fill in the blanks in the pronunciation section for 국립 below.**

국립 [구 ㅂ]  national

Did you fill in the blanks?

Like in 석류 and 국립, when the final consonant ㄱ and the consonant ㄹ meet in succession, the ㄱ should be pronounced as [ㅇ] and the ㄹ should be pronounced as [ㄴ]. It is much easier to pronounce that way.

Both turn into nasal sounds that are articulated from a similar position in your throat.

▶ **Listen to the native speaker's pronunciation and repeat.**

05

석류 [성뉴] pomegranate

국립 [궁닙] national

● **Now, let's look at when the final consonant sound [ㅂ] meets the initial consonant ㄹ.**

As expected, they both change into nasalized sounds. Among the nasal sounds, which sounds could they be changed into? What is the nasal sound that is articulated with your lips in a similar position to ㅂ? What nasal sound has a similar position of articulation to ㄹ?

● **Fill in the blanks in the pronunciation of 입력 and 협력.**

입력 [이 ㅋ] input; entry

협력 [혀 ㅋ] cooperation; collaboration

The final consonant ㅂ that comes before ㄹ is pronounced as [ㅁ], and the ㄹ is pronounced as [ㄴ].

▶ **Listen to the native speaker's pronunciation and follow along.**
06

입력 [임녁] input; entry

협력 [혐녁] cooperation; collaboration

▶ **Let's practice with some other words.**
07

국립대 [궁닙때] national university

목록 [몽녹] list

착륙 [창뉵] landing

확률 [황뉼] probability; chance

합격률 [합꼉뉼] acceptance rate

실업률 [시럼뉼] unemployment rate

취업률 [취:엄뉼] employment rate

독립했어요. [동니패써요.] I've moved out (away from my family).

Quiz Time!

● In each pronunciation section, select the correct pronunciation sound that goes in the blank(s).

Q1.

능력 [능 | 켝] ⓐ ㄹ ⓑ ㄴ ⓒ ㅇ

Q2.

입력 [이 | 녁] ⓐ ㅁ ⓑ ㄴ ⓒ ㅇ

Q3.

독립 [도 | 닙] ⓐ ㄱ, ㄴ ⓑ ㄴ, ㄴ ⓒ ㅇ, ㄴ

Q4.

종류 [종 | ㅠ] ⓐ ㅁ ⓑ ㄴ ⓒ ㅇ

Q5.

국립대 [구 | 닙 | 때]

ⓐ ㅇ, ㄴ

ⓑ ㅇ, ㅁ

ⓒ ㄱ, ㄴ

If the pronunciations of the underlined parts are the same, mark O in the blank. If they are different, mark it with an X.

Q6. ( ) ⓐ **입장료** admission, entrance fee

ⓑ **수수료** commission; fee; charge

Q7. ( ) ⓐ **저녁** evening, dinner

ⓑ **영향력** influence

Q8. ( ) ⓐ **탄산음료** soda, carbonated drink

ⓑ **무료** free; no charge

Q9. ( ) ⓐ **석류** pomegranate

ⓑ **성공** success

Q10. ( ) ⓐ **정류장** stop, station

ⓑ **석류** pomegranate

Q11. (   ) ⓐ **독립** independence

ⓑ **동전** coin

Did you check your answers?

▶ **You can check the native speaker's pronunciation if you would like to.**
Q1~11

Let's practice with sentences!

▶ Paying attention to the parts in bold, read slowly and accurately. Then, listen to the native speaker's pronunciation. Practice faster and faster until you can say them all smoothly!

Q12. **석류**로 만든 **음료수**가 유행이에요.

= Beverages made from pomegranate are popular.

Q13. **독립할 능력** 있어요?

= Are you capable of (leaving home and) living on your own?

Q14. 보통 사립대가 **국립대**보다 **등록금**이 비싸요.

= Usually, private universities are more expensive than national universities.

Q15. **심리학과** 학생들 **취업률**은 어때요?

= What is the employment rate for psychology students?

Q16. **입장료**가 다른 데보다 싸서 **경쟁력**이 있어요.

= The entrance fee is cheaper than other places, so it is competitive.

Answers

Q1. ⓑ	Q5. ⓐ	Q9. O (ⓐ [성뉴] ⓑ [성공])
Q2. ⓐ	Q6. X (ⓐ [입짱뇨] ⓑ [수수료])	Q10. O (ⓐ [정뉴장] ⓑ [성뉴])
Q3. ⓒ	Q7. O (ⓐ [저녁] ⓑ [영:향녁])	Q11. O (ⓐ [동닙] ⓑ [동전])
Q4. ⓑ	Q8. X (ⓐ [탄:산음뇨] ⓑ [무료])	

Lesson 5

ㄴ, *Watch Out for* ㄹ.

What do you think the proper pronunciation of the following word might be?

연락 contact

ⓐ [연낙] ⓑ [연락] ⓒ [열락]

▶ **Listen to the native speaker's pronunciation.**
01

That is right. The answer is c.

Why is that?

The title of this chapter gives us a hint: "ㄴ, Watch Out for ㄹ." When ㄴ meets ㄹ, it always sounds like [ㄹ]. It is easier to pronounce this way.

연 + 락 ⋯→ [열락]

Let's look at another example.

Lunar New Year's Day in Korean is 설날. How should 설날 be pronounced?

설날 Lunar New Year's Day

▶ **Listen to the native speaker's pronunciation.**
02

That is right. It is pronounced as [설:랄]. This word is different from 연락 in that ㄹ comes before ㄴ. However, ㄴ is still next to ㄹ and so is therefore pronounced as [ㄹ].

설 + 날 ⋯ [설:랄]

Let's take a look at some more examples where ㄴ and ㄹ meet, regardless of the order they are in. Listen to the native speaker's pronunciation and follow along.

03

신랑 [실랑] groom

난로 [날:로] heater, stove

줄넘기 [줄럼끼] jump rope

칼날 [칼랄] the blade of a knife

실내 [실래] indoor

겨울날 [겨울랄] winter days

과일나무 [과:일라무] fruit tree

편리해요. [펼리해요] It's convenient.

Great! This time, try reading the expression below.

주말 날씨 weekend weather

(▶) 04 **How did you pronounce it? Listen to the native speaker's pronunciation and pay attention to the change in the pronunciation.**

주말 날씨 ⋯▸ [주말랄씨]

If ㄴ and ㄹ are in succession not only within one word, but also between words like this, then ㄴ is pronounced as [ㄹ].

(▶) 05 **Shall we practice some more?**

일 년 [일련] one year

부를 노래 [부를로래] song to sing

주말 뉴스 [주말류쓰] weekend news

출발 날짜 [출발랄짜] departure date

Quiz Time!

● Taking note of what you learned earlier, read the two dialogues below aloud. Find and mark the places where ㄴ and ㄹ meet and ㄴ is pronounced as [ㄹ].

1.

현우: 다혜 씨, 제주도 갈 날이 얼마 안 남았어요.

= Dahye, it won't be long before we leave for Jeju Island.

다혜: 그러네요. 제주도 가서 어디 가고 싶어요?

= You're right. Where do you want to go on Jeju Island?

현우: 저는 한라산 가고 싶어요. 다혜 씨는요?

= I want to go to Mt. Halla. How about you, Dahye?

다혜: 요즘 너무 추워요. 저는 실내에서 놀고 싶어요.

= It's been too cold recently. I want to hang out inside.

2.

현우: 예지 씨, 내일 생일이에요?

= Yeji, is it your birthday tomorrow?

예지: 네.

= Yes.

현우: 생일날 뭐 할 거예요?

= What are you going to do on your birthday?

예지: 음... 고민 중이에요.

= Umm... I'm thinking.

현우: 그런데 예지 씨, 올해 스물네 살이죠?

= By the way, Yeji, you are 24 this year, right?

예지: 아니요. 일 년 뒤에 스물네 살이에요.

= No. I will turn 24 next year.

● **Check to see if you marked the right places.**

Q1.

현우: 다혜 씨, 제주도 **갈 날**이 얼마 안 남았어요.

다혜: 그러네요. 제주도 가서 어디 가고 싶어요?

현우: 저는 **한라산** 가고 싶어요. 다혜 씨는요?

다혜: 요즘 너무 추워요. 저는 **실내**에서 놀고 싶어요.

현우: 예지 씨, 내일 생일이에요?

예지: 네.

현우: **생일날** 뭐 할 거예요?

예지: 음... 고민 중이에요.

현우: 그런데 예지 씨, 올해 **스물네** 살이죠?

예지: 아니요. **일 년** 뒤에 **스물네** 살이에요.

(▶) Now listen to the native speakers' pronunciation of the conversation. Try to

Q1,Q2 pay attention to the parts where ㄴ is pronounced as [ㄹ].

Listen one more time. This time, say the sentences out loud at the same time as the native speakers.

Lesson 6

The Quiet Strength of ㅎ

● **Read the two words below.**

어떻게 how 어떡해. What are we supposed to do?

(▶) **Listen to the native speaker's pronunciation.**
01

What do you think? Did 어떻게 and 어떡해 sound the same?

That is right. 어떻게 and 어떡해 have the exact same pronunciation. The reason for this is that when the ㄱ and ㅎ sounds are combined, they become a [ㅋ] sound.

어떻게 [어떠케]

어떡해 [어떠캐]

어떻게 and 어떡해 are pronounced as above. The pronunciations of ㅔ and ㅐ are, in theory, different, but in reality the difference is barely perceptible. Therefore, you can look at the two as having the same pronunciation.

In this lesson we will practice examples where the ㅎ sound is combined with ㄱ, ㄷ, ㅂ, ㅅ, or ㅈ.

First, let's look at some examples similar to 어떻게, where ㅎ is the final consonant and the next syllable starts with a ㄱ, ㄷ or ㅈ. ㅎ, therefore making ㄱ, ㄷ, or ㅈ sound stronger and causing the ㅎ sound to disappear. What are stronger sounds, exactly? They are sounds that produce more air when you say them.

$$ㅎ + ㄱ = [ㅋ]$$

$$ㅎ + ㄷ = [ㅌ]$$

$$ㅎ + ㅈ = [ㅊ]$$

Shall we practice with some real expressions? Listen and follow along.

02

좋고 [조:코] It's good and...

좋다! [조:타!] This is good!

이렇게 [이러케] like this

그렇지만 [그러치만] but, however

놓고 왔어요. [노코 와써요.] I left it (somewhere).

빨갛게 [빨:가케] red

그렇대요. [그러태요.] They said so.

How To Sound Like A Native Korean Speaker

This time we will look at some examples where ㄱ, ㄷ, ㅂ, or ㅈ is the final consonant, followed by ㅎ as the first consonant of the next syllable. In these examples as well, ㅎ makes ㄱ, ㄷ, ㅂ, and ㅈ sound stronger, while disappearing itself.

$$ㄱ + ㅎ = [ㅋ]$$

$$ㄷ + ㅎ = [ㅌ]$$

$$ㅂ + ㅎ = [ㅍ]$$

$$ㅈ + ㅎ = [ㅊ]$$

Shall we practice with some real expressions? Listen and repeat.

03

특히 [트키] especially, particularly

길이 막혀요. [기리 마켜요.] There's a lot of traffic.

복잡해요. [복짜패요.] It's complicated.

잡혔어요. [자펴써요.] (Someone) got caught.

한국하고 미국 [한:구카고 미국] Korea and America

급하게 [그파게] in haste

부딪힐 뻔했어요. [부디칠 뻔해써요.] I almost bumped into it.

맞혔어요. [마처써요.] You got it right.

However, in certain instances when ㅈ as a final consonant meets ㅎ, it does not make the [ㅊ] sound but rather the [ㅌ] sound.

 **Let's look at a few examples below.**
04
낮하고 밤 [나타고 밤] day and night

빚하고 세금 [비타고 세:금] debt and tax

This rule applies to words in which a noun ending in the final consonant ㅈ meets a syllable beginning with ㅎ. You can simply think of it as being because when ㅈ is used as a final consonant, it makes the [ㄷ] sound, therefore making the [ㅌ] sound when it meets ㅎ.

Outside of this, ㅅ and ㅊ, both of which are pronounced as [ㄷ] when used as final consonants, are also pronounced as [ㅌ] when the following syllable starts with ㅎ.

꽃향기 [꼬탕기] the scent of a flower

비슷해요. [비스태요.] They are similar.

따뜻한 말 [따뜨탄 말:] warm words

잘못했어요. [잘모태써요.] You did wrong.

아직 못 했어요. [아직 모:태써요.] I haven't been able to do it yet.

노래 잘 못해요. [노래 잘 모:태요.] I can't sing well.

몇 호선 타요? [며토선 타요?] Which subway line do you take?

Therefore, except for when it appears at the very beginning of a word, the consonant ㅎ does not make its own sound, but rather affects, is affected by, or becomes a different sound. In that regard, now can you see how ㅎ is quiet but strong?

Quiz Time!

- Match the consonants on the right with the blanks on the left to make the correct pronunciations of the phrases below.

Q1. 예약했어요.

[예:야⬚애 써요] •

= I made a reservation.

• ㅋ

Q2. 정확하게

[정:화⬚ㅏ게] •

= precisely

• ㅌ

Q3. 답답해요.

[답따⬚애요] •

= It's frustrating.

• ㅍ

Q4. 놓지 마세요.

[노⬚ㅣ마세요] •

= Don't let go of it.

• ㅊ

Q5. 선택했어요.

[선:태⬚애 써요] •

= I made a choice.

⊙ Check your answers with the native speaker's pronunciation. Once you have

Q1~Q5 checked your answers, listen to the native speaker's pronunciation again and repeat.

How To Sound Like A Native Korean Speaker

If the consonants that go in the blanks of the pronunciations for both ⓐ and ⓑ are the same, mark it with an O. If they are different, mark it with an X.

Q6. (   )

ⓐ 티켓하고 ticket and...

[티 | 케 | ㅏ | 고]

ⓑ 낮하고 day and...

[나 | ㅏ | 고]

Q7. (   )

ⓐ 꽃향기 the scent of a flower

[꼬 | ㅑ | 기]

ⓑ 옷 한 벌 a piece of clothing

[오 | ㅏ | 벌]

Q8. (   )

ⓐ 깨끗해요. It's clean.

[깨 | 끄 | ㅐ | 요]

ⓑ 맞혀 보세요. Take a guess.

[마 | ㅓ | 보 | 세 | 요]

Q9. (   )

ⓐ 꽂혔어요. I'm hooked on it.

[꼬 | ㅓ | 써 | 요]

ⓑ 꽃이에요. It's a flower.

[꼬 | ㅣ | 에 | 요]

▶ Check your answers with the native speaker's pronunciation. Once you have checked your answers, listen to the native speaker's pronunciation again and repeat.

Q6~Q9

Let's practice with sentences!

▶ Read the sentences below slowly. Then practice again faster and faster.

Q10. 꽃향기 진짜 좋다!

= The scent of the flowers is so nice!

Q11. 어떻게 가는지 정확하게 알아볼게요.

= I'll find out exactly how to get there.

Q12. 비행기 티켓하고 호텔, 다 예약했어요?

= Did you reserve both the plane ticket and the hotel?

Q13. 제가 요즘 뭐에 꽂혔는지 맞혀 보세요.

= Guess what I've been stuck on recently.

Q14. 한국하고 미국, 이렇게 가 봤어요.

= I've been to Korea and America.

Answers

Q1. ㅋ	Q4. ㅊ	Q7. O ([꼬턍기], [오탄벌])
Q2. ㅋ	Q5. ㅋ	Q8. X ([깨끄태요], [마처보세요])
Q3. ㅍ	Q6. O ([티케타고], [나타고])	Q9. O ([꼬처써요], [꼬치에요])

Lesson 7 - 1

Sticky Consonants

● Read the two words below. If the pronunciations of both are the same, write O. If their pronunciations are different, write X. (   )

같이 together with, like (something)   가치 value; worth

▶ Find out if the pronunciations of the two words are the same or different by
01 checking the native speaker's pronunciation.

Did you check? Just as the native speaker pronounced them, 같이 and 가치 are both pronounced [가치]. Did you mark them correctly as being the same? Or, in the case of 같이, did you think that the final consonant ㅌ moves to the next syllable and is pronounced [가티]?

Take a guess at how the word below is pronounced.

굳이 obstinately

[구디]? [구치]? Or "[구찌] (GUCCI)"?

▶ Listen to the native speaker's pronunciation.
02

Although it seems like the final consonant ㄷ should be moved to the following syllable to be pronounced as [구디], the native speaker actually pronounced it as [구지].

In this lesson, we will practice this phenomenon of pronouncing the final consonants ㄷ and ㅌ as [ㅈ] or [ㅊ] when combined with the vowel ㅣ in a postposition or suffix.

Before that, let's take a look first at what combines to make 같이 and 굳이.

같이 = 같(다) to be like + -이

굳이 = 굳(다) to be firm + -이

That's right. The -이 in 같이 and 굳이 is a suffix that creates an adverb.

This time, let's practice examples where we combine a word stem that ends with the final consonant ㄷ or ㅌ with the suffix -이 to make a noun.

03

해돋이 [해도지] sunrise (해가 돋(다) sun rises + -이)

여닫이 [여:다지] hinged door (여닫(다) to open and close + -이)

미닫이 [미:다지] sliding door (밀어서 닫(다) to slide and close + -이)

Now, let's practice with examples of a noun that ends with a ㄷ or a ㅌ consonant and the subject marking particle -이.

04

끝이 [끄치] the end is... (끝 end + -이)

햇볕이 [핻뼈치] sunshine is... (햇볕 sunshine + -이)

바깥이 [바까치] outside is... (바깥 outside + -이)

머리숱이 [머리수치] one's hair thickness is...

(머리숱 one's hair thickness [in terms of the number of strands] + -이)

Lesson 7 - 2

Morphing Consonants

● Read the two words below, and if the way they are pronounced is the same, write O. If their pronunciations are different, write X. (   )

닫히다 to be closed   **다치다** to get hurt/injured

(▶) Find out if the pronunciations of the two words are the same or different by
05 checking the native speaker's pronunciation.

Did you listen? What do you think? They are pronounced the same way, [다치 다], right?

Isn't it strange? In the previous lesson, Chapter 4 Lesson 6, we learned that when the final consonant ㄷ and the ㅎ initial consonant meet, it makes the [ㅌ] sound.

However, in this lesson, we will look at the exceptional cases in which ㄷ and ㅎ meet and are changed to [ㅊ] instead of [ㅌ]. When the affix -히- follows the final consonant [ㄷ], it becomes [ㅊ]. The affix -히- adds a passive or a causative meaning to the word. The word that we read above, 닫히다, is the passive expression of "닫다 (= to close)".

$$닫히다 = 닫(다) + -히- + -다$$

                  to close, to shut   suffix

▶ 06 Let's look at and practice some more examples where the final consonant ㄷ and the affix −히− are combined.

닫히다 [다치다] to be closed

갇히다 [가치다] to be locked up

묻히다 [무치다] to be buried

굳히다 [구치다] to harden, to solidify

걷히다 [거치다] to be put away, to be cleared away

▶ 07 Did you listen to the native speaker and follow along? The expressions we practiced above are in standard form, so this time let's add the past tense form −었어요 and practice.

닫혔어요. [다처써요.] It's closed.

갇혔어요. [가처써요.] I'm stuck/trapped.

묻혔어요. [무처써요.] It's buried.

굳혔어요. [구처써요.] I hardened/solidified it.

걷혔어요. [거처써요.] It's been cleared away.

The pronunciations of all the expressions above are written as [처써요] rather than [쳤어요]. This is because when the vowel ㅕ combines with the consonant ㅊ, it does not make the ㅕ sound, but rather the ㅓ sound.

Pop Quiz!

● Let's review while answering the quiz questions.

Q1. Select the word(s) in which the first sound of the second syllable is pronounced as [ㅈ].

　ⓐ 꽃이 flower is...
　ⓑ 볕이 sunlight is...
　ⓒ 굳이 obstinately
　ⓓ 굳히다 to harden

Q2. Select the one(s) where the first sound of the second syllable is NOT pronounced as [ㅊ].

　ⓐ 닫았어요. I closed it.
　ⓑ 닫혔어요. It's closed.
　ⓒ 갇혔어요. I'm stuck.
　ⓓ 같이 together with

Q3. Select the one(s) where the first sound of the second syllable is pronounced as [ㅊ].

　ⓐ 숱이 the amount (of hair) is...
　ⓑ 같은 same
　ⓒ 걷었어요. I put it away.
　ⓓ 끝이에요. It's the end.

▶ **Check the pronunciation of the expressions from the questions.**
Q1~Q3

Let's practice with sentences!

▶ Listen to the native speaker's pronunciation and practice slowly and accurately first, then practice saying it faster.

Q4. **같이** 하니까 **끝이** 보이네요.

= Since we're working together, I can see the finish line.

Q5. **해돋이** 보러 **굳이** 거기까지 가야 돼요?

= Do we really need to go that far just to see the sunrise?

Q6. 이 팩은 **붙이는** 거예요, 바르고 **굳히는** 거예요?

= Is this face mask the type that you stick on, or the type that you spread on and let dry?

Q7. 바깥에 구름이 **걷혔어요.**

= The clouds have cleared outside.

Q8. 이 문은 **여닫이문**이에요, **미닫이문**이에요?

= Is this door a swinging door or a sliding door?

Answers

Q1. ⓒ Q2. ⓐ Q3. ⓐ, ⓓ

Real Experiences by Korean Learners

This anecdote shared by 트리스, USA

'맹고' 님 맞죠?

맹고???

안녕, 난 이제부터 '맹고'야.

I used to hang out with some Korean friends I met through a 단톡방 (group chat), and sometimes we met in person to either go for drinks or hang out. We all had nicknames, and sometimes I didn't know who was who. So when I first met this person with the nickname 망고 in the chat, I asked her if she was 맹고 (how English speakers pronounce mango) from the group chat. She had no idea what I was saying until I realized that I was saying it wrong. All of the people in the 단톡방 thought it was hilarious and started calling her 맹고 님, and she eventually changed her name in the group chat.

CHAPTER 5

읽 Wherefore Art Thou Pronounced 익?

● Read the two expressions below aloud.

젊고 young and...

젊어요. He/she is young.

▶ Check the native speaker's pronunciation.

01

What do you think? Was your pronunciation correct? Or were you wrong?

젊고 [점:꼬]

젊어요. [절머요.]

When 젊고 is pronounced, the ㄹ in the final consonant block ㄿ disappears, but when saying 젊어요, the final consonant block ㄿ is split into two sounds.

In this lesson, we will practice the pronunciation of final consonants that contain two consonants as combined final consonant blocks. There are a total of 11 combined final consonant blocks in Korean (ㄳ, ㄵ, ㄼ, ㄽ, ㄾ, ㅄ, ㄺ, ㄻ, ㄿ, ㅀ, ㅀ), but in this lesson, we will practice only the eight most frequently used blocks.

First, let's look at what happens when a syllable ending in a combined final consonant block is followed by a vowel. In these cases, like in "젊어요 [절머요]", the first consonant in the block is pronounced as the final consonant, while the second consonant in the block is pronounced as the first sound of the following syllable.

▶ Shall we practice?

젊어요. [절머요.] He/she is young.

젊은 사람 [절믄 사람] young person

젊었을 때 [절머쓸 때] when I was young

▶ Shall we practice with some more words?

(ㄹㄱ)
읽어요. [일거요.] I read it.
맑아요. [말가요.] It's clear.

(ㄵ)
앉으세요. [안즈세요.] Have a seat.

(ㄹㅂ)
넓어요. [널버요.] It's spacious.
밟았어요. [발바써요.] I stepped on it.

(ㄹㅁ)
삶은 계란 [살믄 계란] boiled egg
삶이란... [살:미란] Life is...

(ㄹㅌ)
훑어보세요. [훌터보세요.] Skim through it.

(ㅄ)
없어요. [업:써요.]* I don't have it. / It's not there.
값이 비싸요. [갑씨 비싸요.]* It's expensive.

* Like we learned in Chapter 4 Lesson 1, if ㅅ comes after the final consonant
sound [ㅂ], the ㅅ is pronounced as [ㅆ].

Did you practice enough?

Now, let's take a look at some exceptions. **For the combined final consonant blocks ᅝ and ᆶ, even when they are followed by a vowel the ㅎ does not combine with that vowel. The ㅎ just disappears.**

▶ 04 **Listen to how the native speaker pronounces the two expressions below.**

괜찮아요. I'm okay.

싫어해요. I hate it.

That is right. The ㅎ disappears and the remaining consonant combines with the vowel following it.

괜찮아요. [괜차나요.]

싫어해요. [시러해요.]

▶ 05 **Shall we practice with some other expressions as well?**

많아요. [마:나요.] There's a lot.

그렇지 않아요. [그러치 아나요.] That's not true.

있잖아요. [일짜나요.] You know what?

물 끓어요. [물 끄러요.] The water is boiling.

잃어버렸어요. [이러버려써요.] I've lost it.

끊임없이 [끄니멉씨] constantly, ceaselessly

Once you have practiced enough, let's take a look at <u>cases where the combined consonant blocks are followed by another consonant</u>.

In these cases, only one out of the two consonants in the combined consonant block is pronounced. Which one gets pronounced out of the two?

● **As you read, try marking which consonant of the two is pronounced as the final consonant.**

읽(다) to read

없(다) to not have, to not exist, to be not there

앉(다) to sit

젊(다) to be young

많(다) to be a lot

싫(다) to hate

짧(다) to be short

▶ Did you mark all of them? Now, listen to the native speaker's pronunciation and check your answers.

읽다 [익따]

없다 [업:따]

앉다 [안따]

젊다 [점:따]

많다 [만:타]

싫다 [실타]

짧다 [짤따]

There are no set rules for which consonant in a combined consonant block is pronounced and which is not, so all you can do is memorize each one. Rather than memorizing it as, for example, "in the combined final consonant block 리, the ㄱ is pronounced", try to memorize it as "읽다 is pronounced as [익따]".

● **Now, let's take some time to memorize.**

Did you memorize them all? If so, let's take a quiz.

● **Fill in the blank with the consonant that is pronounced out of the combined final consonant block.**

긁다 [그□따]

삶다 [사:따]

넓다 [너따]

늙다 [늑따]

귀찮다 [귀차타]

닮다 [다:따]

닭고기 [다꼬기]

▶ Did you finish? Listen to the native speaker's pronunciation and check your
07 answers.

굵다 [극따]

삶다 [삼:따]

넓다 [널따]

늙다 [늑따]

귀찮다 [귀찬타]

닮다 [담:따]

닭고기 [닥꼬기]

● **Read them out loud several times to get used to the sounds.**

You may have noticed when looking at the pronunciation of "많다 [만:타]", "싫다 [실타]", and "귀찮다 [귀찬타]", that the ㅎ does not completely disappear, but rather affects the initial sound of the following syllable. So, like we learned in Chapter 4 Lesson 6, ㅎ changes the pronunciation so that ㄱ becomes [ㅋ], ㄷ becomes [ㅌ], and ㅈ becomes [ㅊ].

● **Read the expressions below aloud.**

너무 많지 않아요?
= Don't you think there are too many?

다혜 씨가 싫대요.
= Dahye said she doesn't want to.

귀찮겠지만 해야 돼요.
= It must be a pain in the neck, but you have to do it.

▶ **Listen to the native speaker's pronunciation.**
08

[너무 만:치 아나요?]

[다혜 씨가 실태요.]

[귀찬켙찌만 해야 돼요.]

It would be nice if we could finish off here, but as usual, there are some exceptions. Let's practice some exceptions that differ from what we learned above.

1. ㄹㄱ

When the combined final consonant block ㄹㄱ is followed by another consonant, which consonant did we say gets pronounced? That is right. ㄱ is pronounced. However, there is an exception to this rule when the ㄹㄱ final consonant is followed by a word ending that begins with ㄱ. When this happens, the ㄹ is pronounced as the final consonant, rather than the ㄱ. (In the word 닭고기, however, 고기 is not a word ending but is part of the word, so the correct pronunciation is [닥꼬기], not [달꼬기].)

● **Read the expressions below aloud.**

책 읽기 싫어요. I don't want to read a book.

등 긁고 있어요. I'm scratching my back.

▶ **Listen to the native speaker's pronunciation.**

09

[책 일끼 시러요.]

[등 글꼬 이써요.]

2. ㄼ

When the combined final consonant block ㄼ is followed by another consonant, which consonant did we say gets pronounced? That is right. ㄹ is pronounced. However, there is one word where the ㅂ is pronounced as the final consonant sound — 밟다! The 밟 of the word 밟다 is not pronounced as [발:], but rather as [밥:]. 밟다 means "to step on".

● **Read the expressions below aloud.**

밟고 갔어요. He stepped on it.

밟지 마세요. Don't step on it.

▶ **Listen to the native speaker's pronunciation.**
10

[밥:꼬 가써요.]

[밥:찌 마세요.]

Let's practice through dialogues!

This time, let's practice pronouncing the combined final consonant blocks using the following dialogues. First, write the pronunciation of the expressions that contain combined final consonant blocks in the blanks.

1.

A: 머리 **짧게** 자르고 싶어요.

　　　[　　]

B: 보람 씨는 **짧은** 머리도 잘 어울릴 거 같아요.

[   ]

A: I want to cut my hair short.

B: I think short hair would also suit you, Boram.

2.

A: 저기 **넓은** 데 가서 **앉는** 게 어때요?

[   ]   [   ]

B: 저기는 벌레 **많은데** 그냥 여기 **앉으면** 안 돼요?

[   ]   [   ]

A: What do you think about going over and sitting in that wide open area?

B: There are a lot of bugs over there. Can't we just sit here?

3.

A: 배고픈데 라면 **끓여** 먹자.

[   ]

B: 라면은 **없고** 계란은 있는데, 계란 **삶아** 먹을래?

[   ]   [   ]

A: I'm hungry. Let's make some ramyeon.

B: We don't have ramyeon, but we do have eggs. Do you want to boil and eat some eggs?

4.

A: 어젯밤에 그 책 다 **읽고** 잤어요?

[   ]

B: 아니요. **읽다가** 잠들었어요.

[   ]

A: Did you read that whole book before sleeping last night?

B: No. I fell asleep while I was reading it.

5.

A: 우와! 가게가 진짜 **밝네요.**

[   ]

B: 네. 가게가 **넓지 않아서** 조명을 **많이** 설치했어요.

[   ][   ]   [   ]

A: Wow! The shop is so bright.

B: Yeah. The shop isn't very big so we installed lots of lights.

Answers

1. [짤께], [짤븐]

2. [널븐], [안는], [마:는데], [안즈면]

3. [끄려], [업:꼬], [살마]

4. [일꼬], [익따가]

5. [방네요]*, [널찌], [아나서], [마:니]

* If you are wondering why it is not [박네요], check out Chapter 4 Lesson 3.

▶ Did you come up with the correct pronunciations? Now, listen to the native
11 speaker's pronunciation and follow along.

CHAPTER 6.

What?! I Did Not Know It Would Sound Like This!

Lesson 1

Why Isn't 겉옷 Pronounced [거톤]?

● **Read the word below.**

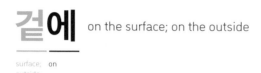

겉에 on the surface; on the outside

surface; on
outside

▶ **Check the native speaker's pronunciation.**

01

That is right. If a final consonant is followed by a syllable beginning with a
vowel, that vowel is pronounced using that consonant. So, 겉에 is pronounced
as [거테].

So, then, how would you read the word below?

겉옷 outer clothing

surface; clothes
outside

▶ **Check the native speaker's pronunciation.**

02

What do you think? How did they pronounce it?
That is right. They pronounced it as [거돋] instead of [거톤]. Let's learn why in
this lesson.

The reason 겉옷 is pronounced as [거돋] and not [거톧] is because 겉옷 has been made by combining two words into one.

As you know, when ㅌ is used as a final consonant, it is pronounced as [ㄷ].

What are the consonants that are pronounced as [ㄷ]?

ㄷ, ㅅ, ㅆ, ㅈ, ㅊ, ㅌ, ㅎ

When these consonants are used as the final consonant in a syllable, they make the [ㄷ] sound.

For example, take the following.

03

꽃 [꼳] flower

맛 [맏] taste, flavor

끝 [끋] end, finish

But what happens if we add a postpositional particle?

04

꽃을 [꼬츨]

맛이 [마시]

끝에 [끄테]

How To Sound Like A Native Korean Speaker

As you can see, the original consonant sound is pronounced as is.

However, when a word with a stand-alone meaning is added, such as in 겉옷, the final consonants ㅌ, ㅅ, ㅆ, ㅈ, ㅊ, ㅎ are pronounced as [ㄷ], and this sound is carried over to the first sound of the second part of the word.

윗옷 [위돋] upper (clothing)

upper   clothes

맛없다 [마덥따] to be not tasty

taste   it does not exist

This is the case not only for single words, but also for phrases that are pronounced like a single word.

● **Try pronouncing the following expressions.**

옷 안에 under the clothes

못 왔어요. I couldn't come.

몇 월에요? In what month?

Listen to the native speaker's pronunciation and follow along.

옷 안에 [오다네]

못 왔어요. [모:돠써요.]

몇 월에요? [며둬레요?]

This is true not only for consonants that are pronounced as [ㄷ] when used as a final consonant, but also for the final consonants ㅋ and ㅍ as well, which are pronounced as [ㄱ] and [ㅂ] respectively.

- **Try pronouncing the following expressions.**

앞에 in front of

앞 아파트에 in the apartment across from (someone)

부엌에 in the kitchen

부엌 안에 inside the kitchen

▶ **Listen and check the native speaker's pronunciation.**
07

앞에 [아페]

앞 아파트에 [아바파트에]

부엌에 [부어케]

부엌 안에 [부어가네]

Let's practice through dialogues!

Listen to the conversations, and pay attention to which final consonants simply move to the first sound of the following syllable, and which final consonants are changed to [ㅂ], [ㄷ], or [ㄱ] first.

▶ 1.
08
A: 어머, 다혜 씨, 이 동네 살아요?

= Oh, Dahye, do you live in this neighborhood?

B: 네. 앞 아파트로 이사 왔어요.

= Yes. I moved to the apartment across the way.

A: 몇 월에요?

= When? (Literal: In what month?)

B: 3월에 이사 오려고 했었는데, 사정이 있어서 못 오고, 며칠 전에 왔어요.

= I planned to move in March, but I couldn't due to the circumstances, so I moved here a few days ago.

2.

A: 은희 씨, 겉에 입은 옷 멋지네요.

= Eun-hee, your outerwear is nice.

B: 감사합니다. 주말에 겉옷 몇 벌 샀어요.

= Thank you. I bought some outerwear over the weekend.

A: 옷 안에 그건 뭐예요?

= What's that you've got inside?

B: 이 앞에서 산 꽃이에요. 준배 씨 주려고 가져왔어요.

= It's a flower I bought nearby. I bought it to give to you, Joonbae.

Now listen to the native speaker again and read along.

1ʹ.

A: 어머, 다혜 씨, 이 동네 살아요?

[사라요?]

B: 네. 앞 아파트로 이사 왔어요.
     [아바파트로]   [와써요.]

A: 몇 월에요?
     [머둬레요?]

B: 3월에 이사 오려고 했었는데, 사정이 있어서 못 오고,
     [사뭐레]   [해썬는데]   [이써서 모:도고,]
  며칠 전에 왔어요.
       [저네 와써요.]

2'.

A: 은희 씨, 겉에 입은 옷 멋지네요.
    [으니]   [거테 입으논 먿찌네요.]

B: 감사합니다. 주말에 겉옷 몇 벌 샀어요.
    [감:사함니다. 주마레 거돈몓뻘 사써요.]

A: 옷 안에 그건 뭐예요?
    [오다네]

B: 이 앞에서 산 꽃이에요. 준배 씨 주려고 가져왔어요.
     [아페서]   [꼬치에요.]   [가저와써요.]

Lesson 2

Why Isn't 꽃잎 Pronounced [꼬칩]?

● **Read the word below.**

꽃잎 petal

How did you read it?
[꼬칩]?
[꼬딥]?

 **Check the native speaker's pronunciation.**
01

That is right. 꽃잎 is pronounced as [꼰닙].
Why is it not pronounced as [꼬칩] or [꼬딥], but as [꼰닙]?

꽃잎 is a word made by combining "꽃 (= flower)" and "잎 (= leaf)". When two or more words are combined to form a word or a phrase, if there is a final consonant at the end of the previous word and the next word starts with 이, 야, 여, 요, 유, 얘, or 예, then you usually add [ㄴ]. They are then pronounced as [니], [냐], [녀], [뇨], [뉴], [냬], and [녜].

꽃 + 잎 = 꽃잎   이, 야, 여, 요, 유, 얘, 예

Final consonant

[꼰닙]   [니, 냐, 녀, 뇨, 뉴, 냬, 녜]

Why is 꽃 pronounced as [꼰]? This is because the final consonant, ㅊ, is pronounced as [ㄷ], and when ㄷ is followed by ㄴ, ㄷ is pronounced as [ㄴ].

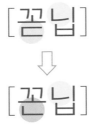

$$[꼳닙]$$

⇩

$$[꼰닙]$$

If you do not quite understand why the final consonant ㄷ is pronounced as [ㄴ], you can go back to Chapter 4 Lesson 3 and practice.

In addition to 꽃잎, the words 깻잎 and 나뭇잎 are also pronounced similarly. How might you say these two words?

깻잎 perilla leaf   나뭇잎 leaf

▶ **Listen to the native speaker.**
02

That is right. 깻잎 is pronounced [깬닙], and 나뭇잎 is pronounced [나문닙].

▶ **Of course, if a vowel comes after 꽃잎, 깻잎, and 나뭇잎, the final consonant,**
03 **ㅍ, will be pronounced as is.**

꽃잎을 [꼰니플]

깻잎이 [깬니피]

나뭇잎은 [나문니픈]

If that is the case, then how would the word "색연필 (= colored pencil)" be pronounced? 색연필 is a combination of the words 색 and 연필.

색연필

04 ▶ **Listen to the audio to see if the pronunciation you are thinking of is correct.**

That is right. 색연필 is pronounced [생년필].

Since there is a final consonant in the first word and the next word starts with 여, 여 becomes [녀].

색 + 연필 = 색연필   이, 야, 여, 요, 유, 얘, 예

Final consonant

[색년필]   [니, 냐, 녀, 뇨, 뉴, 냬, 녜]

However, [색년필] is difficult to pronounce.

So, as you learned in Chapter 4 Lesson 3, when ㄴ comes after the ㄱ final consonant, you can pronounce the ㄱ as [ㅇ].

[색년필] ⇨ [생년필]

So, then, how should we pronounce 서울역, which means "Seoul Station"?

서울역

Listen to the audio to see if the pronunciation you are thinking of is correct.

Yes. 서울역 is pronounced as [서울력].

"Seoul Station" is a compound word that combines 서울 and 역. However, the word 서울 has a final consonant, and the next word 역 starts with 여, so 역 is pronounced as [녁]. As we learned in Chapter 4 Lesson 5, when ㄴ comes after the ㄹ final consonant, the ㄴ is pronounced as [ㄹ], so [서울녁] changes once more to become [서울력].

[서울역] ⇨ [서울녁] ⇨ [서울력]

All of the words that we have covered so far are compound words that are comprised of two words that can also be used alone.

꽃잎 petal = 꽃 flower + 잎 leaf

깻잎 perilla leaf = (들)깨 perilla seeds + 잎 leaf

나뭇잎 leaf = 나무 tree + 잎 leaf

색연필 colored pencil = 색 color + 연필 pencil

서울역 Seoul Station = 서울 Seoul + 역 station

The same is true for not just these types of compound words, but also for derivatives that combine a word with a prefix. Shall we look at some examples?

한여름 midsummer = **한–** the peak + **여름** summer

늦여름 late summer = **늦–** late + **여름** summer

▶ **How are these two words pronounced? Check out the audio to see if the**
06 **pronunciation you are thinking of is correct.**

Yes. 한여름 is pronounced as [한녀름] and 늦여름 is pronounced as [는녀름].

▶ **As always, there are exceptions.**
07

맛있다 [마싣따 or 마딛따] to be tasty

멋있다 [머싣따 or 머딛따] to look cool

첫인상 [처딘상] first impression

The above words are compounds of two words that make one word. The second word in each compound begins with the vowel 이, but the [ㄴ] sound was still not added, right?

So, it is not a very good method to just look at every word, check to see if it is a compound word, what the first syllable of the second part is, and how it is pronounced. Doing it this way every time will just give you a headache!

You just need to know the rule you have learned in this lesson so that you can say, "Oh! That's it. That is why the [ㄴ] sound is added." We recommend that you just try to pronounce many words aloud as much as possible. That way, you will remember the sound, and it will become a habit so you can pronounce it automatically.

Then, shall we read more words aloud? First, for each word, guess which of the three examples is the correct pronunciation.

1. 물약 liquid medicine

ⓐ [물략] ⓑ [물냑] ⓒ [무략]

2. 알약 tablet, pill

ⓐ [아략] ⓑ [알냑] ⓒ [알략]

3. 기침약 cough medicine

ⓐ [기치먁] ⓑ [기침냑] ⓒ [기침먁]

4. 두통약 headache pill/tablet

ⓐ [두통냑] ⓑ [두통약]

5. 배낭여행 backpacking

ⓐ [배:낭여행] ⓑ [배:낭녀행]

6. 신혼여행 honeymoon

ⓐ [신호녀행] ⓑ [신혼녀행]

7. 어학연수 language study abroad

ⓐ [어:하견수] ⓑ [어:항년수]

ⓒ [어:한년수] ⓓ [어:학년수]

Answers

1. ⓐ   2. ⓒ   3. ⓑ   4. ⓐ   5. ⓑ   6. ⓑ   7. ⓑ

▶ **Did you get them all right? Now, listen and repeat.**
08

So far, we have looked at words only. Shall we look at some phrases this time? As mentioned at the beginning of the lesson, it is easy to see that the [ㄴ] sound is added not only when two or more words are combined to form a single word, but also when forming phrases.

● **Let's read the expressions below.**

미국 영화 American movies

저녁 약속 dinner plans

다음 역 next station

집 열쇠 house key

춤 연습 dance practice

할 일 something to do; business

▶ **Listen to the native speaker, and repeat the words.**
09

미국 영화 [미궁녕화]

저녁 약속 [저녕냑쏙]

다음 역 [다음녁]

집 열쇠 [짐녈쐬]

춤 연습 [춤년습]

할 일 [할릴]

These expressions may contain two separate words rather than one word, but even so they are pronounced as if they were one word, which is why the [ㄴ] sound is added.

● **Choose how the following expressions should be pronounced.**

1. 십육 sixteen (Sino-Korean number)

ⓐ [시뷱]　　　　　ⓑ [십뉵]　　　　　ⓒ [심뉵]

2. 열여섯 sixteen (native Korean number)

ⓐ [열려섣]　　　　ⓑ [열녀섣]　　　　ⓒ [여려섣]

3. 삼십육 thirty-six (Sino-Korean number)

ⓐ [삼시뷱]　　　　ⓑ [삼심뉵]　　　　ⓒ [삼십뉵]

4. 서른여섯 thirty-six (native Korean number)

ⓐ [서른녀섣]　　　ⓑ [서르녀섣]

5. 볼일 something to do; business

    ⓐ [보:릴]   ⓑ [볼:닐]   ⓒ [볼:릴]

6. 옷 입어요. Put on your clothes.

    ⓐ [옫니버요.]   ⓑ [온니버요.]   ⓒ [오시버요.]

7. 안 예뻐요. It is not pretty.

    ⓐ [아녜뻐요.]   ⓑ [안녜뻐요.]

8. 못 읽어요. I can't read.

    ⓐ [몬:닐거요.]   ⓑ [몯:닐거요.]   ⓒ [모:실거요.]

9. 무슨 일이에요? What's happened?

    ⓐ [무스니:리에요?]   ⓑ [무슨니:리에요?]

10. 오늘 무슨 요일이에요? What day is it today?

    ⓐ [오늘무슨뇨이리에요?]   ⓑ [오늘무스뇨이리에요?]

> ***Answers***
>
> 1. ⓒ 2. ⓐ 3. ⓑ 4. ⓐ 5. ⓒ 6. ⓑ 7. ⓑ 8. ⓐ 9. ⓑ 10. ⓐ

▶ Did you get them all right? Now, listen and repeat.

10

* In the case of number 6, "옷 입어요", and number 8, "못 읽어요", some people pronounce them as [오디버요] and [모:딜거요] by applying the rules we learned in Lesson 1.

Lastly, let's practice with dialogue composed of the words we learned earlier.
First, read the dialogue below and then mark the places where the [ㄴ] or [ㄹ]
sound is added.

1.

A: 기침약 사 왔어요?

= Did you buy the cough medicine?

B: 네. 여기요.

= Yes. Here you go.

A: 어? 알약이네요?

= Huh? They're pills?

B: 네. 왜요?

= Yes. Why?

A: 저는 물약이 더 좋은데...

= I like liquid medicine more ...

2.

A: 날씨가 한여름 같네요.

= The weather feels like it is the peak of summer.

B: 그러게요. 오늘 최고 기온 삼십육 도래요.

= It does. They say the high today is thirty-six degrees.

A: 아! 그래서 이렇게 덥구나. 오늘 춤 연습 하는 날인데...

= Ah! So that's why it's so hot. But today is dance practice...

3.

A: 은희 씨, 이 나뭇잎 그려진 옷 어때요?

= What do you think about these clothes with the leaf print, Eunhee?

B: 별로 안 예뻐요.

= They are not very pretty.

A: 그래요? 오늘 저녁 약속에 입고 가려고 했는데...

= Really? I was going to wear them out tonight...

B: 아! 오늘 약속 있어요? 어디서요?

= Ah! You have plans today? Where at?

A: 서울역에서 친구 만나기로 했어요.

= I planned to meet a friend at Seoul Station.

B: 오! 그럼 같이 가요. 저도 서울역에 볼일 있어요.

= Oh! Then let's go together. I also have things to do at Seoul Station.

● Did you mark them all? Check if you marked the right places. Then, listen to and repeat the pronunciation of a native speaker.

(▶) 1'.
11
A: **기침약** 사 왔어요?

B: 네. 여기요.

A: 어? **알약**이네요?

B: 네. 왜요?

A: 저는 **물약**이 더 좋은데...

(▶) 2'.
12
A: 날씨가 **한여름** 같네요.

B: 그러게요. 오늘 최고 기온 **삼십육** 도래요.

A: 아! 그래서 이렇게 덥구나. 오늘 **춤 연습** 하는 날인데...

A: 은희 씨, 이 **나뭇잎** 그려진 옷 어때요?

B: 별로 **안 예뻐요**.

A: 그래요? 오늘 **저녁 약속**에 입고 가려고 했는데...

B: 아! **오늘 약속*** 있어요? 어디서요?

A: **서울역**에서 친구 만나기로 했어요.

B: 오! 그럼 같이 가요. 저도 **서울역**에 **볼일** 있어요.

* 오늘 약속 can be pronounced either as [오늘략쏙] or [오느략쏙].

CHAPTER 7.

Why Don't I Sound Right?

Lesson 1

What Is the Difference Between G and ㄱ?

● Read the word below aloud.

가구 [a- u]

▶ Listen to the native speaker's pronunciation.

01

How would you write ㄱ in romanization?

When ㄱ is romanized, it is usually written as *g* or *k* because ㄱ is similar in sound to both *g* and *k*. In fact, the position of the tongue when pronouncing ㄱ

is almost the same as the position of the tongue when pronouncing *g* or *k*. You pronounce both by placing the back of your tongue on the roof of your mouth and then releasing it.

However, while the pronunciations are similar, they are not exactly the same. ㄱ is pronounced differently from both *g* and *k*. In particular, there is a big difference between *g* and ㄱ. This is because *g* is a voiced sound made by vibrating the vocal cords, but ㄱ is unvoiced. In this way, ㄱ can be seen as more similar to *k* than to *g*.

(Unsure about the difference between voiced and unvoiced sounds? To put it simply, voiced sounds are produced by making a sound with the throat. Unvoiced sounds are sounds that do not produce a sound in the throat, but are made through exhaling air from the mouth.)

Have you ever imagined making a *g* sound while trying to pronounce ㄱ? If you have, try thinking of making a *k* sound instead, but with less air exhaled than usual. If you exhale too much air, it will sound like ㅋ.

We learned the difference between ㄱ and ㅋ in Chapter 1 Lesson 1, right?

When the vowel ㅡ is added to ㄱ and ㅋ, they are pronounced as 그 and 크. 그 sounds lower in tone than 크 and less air is exhaled.

Let's practice by first pronouncing 크 and then changing it to 그.

● **Try pronouncing them in this order.**

크 크 그 그
크 크 그 그

ㅋ ㄱ

ㅋ ㄱ

ㄱ ㄱ

▶ Was it difficult? Listen to the native speaker's pronunciation and follow along.
02

Did you practice it a few more times? How is it now?

If you compare pronouncing *g* in English and pronouncing ㄱ in Korean, when you pronounce ㄱ, you use a lot less force with your tongue and throat.

▶ This time, let's practice by attaching different vowels.
03

가 가 게 게

거 거 기 기

고 고 구 구

겨 겨 과 과

Now, let's practice with words and expressions that use ㄱ. First, we have expressions with ㄱ as the first sound of the first syllable.

Listen and repeat the native speaker's pronunciation. Be careful not to pronounce ㄱ like *g* or ㅋ!

강아지 puppy

검은색 black

걱정 worry, concern

겨울 winter

경험 experience

구십 ninety

그렇게 like that

가능해요. It is possible.

고장 났어요. It is broken.

그만! Stop!

This time, we will practice expressions where ㄱ is in both the first and second syllables.

Before practicing, could you tell that the sound of the first ㄱ and the second ㄱ were different when listening to the native speaker's pronunciation of 가구 at the beginning of this lesson?

When ㄱ is pronounced between two vowels, or between the nasal sounds ㄴ, ㅁ, or ㅇ and a vowel, the vocal cords are engaged. If you thought that the two ㄱ in 가구 sounded different, that is why.

In English especially, *g* and *k* are distinguished by the presence or absence of vocal cord engagement. Because of this, some English-speaking learners may have thought that the sounds were different.

However, even if you did not notice any difference, it does not matter. You do not need to pronounce the ㄱ in the first syllable and the ㄱ in the second syllable differently. In fact, depending on the person speaking and the speed at which they speak, the vocal cords are sometimes engaged and sometimes not.

(▶) **Now, let's practice pronunciation while reading the words below aloud.**
05

가게 shop; store

거기 there

그거 it, that

개구리 frog

공기 air

건강 health

가격 price

감기 걸렸어요. I've caught a cold.

Let's practice with sentences!

Shall we practice by putting the words we have learned into sentences? First, read them to yourself slowly. Then, practice by listening to and repeating the native speaker's pronunciation.

(▶) 그 가격에 가능해요.
06
↳ [그 가겨게 가:능해요.]

= It's possible at that price.

How To Sound Like A Native Korean Speaker

▶ 검은색 옷은 이제 그만!

07

↳ [거믄색 오슨 이제 그만!]

= No more black clothing from now on!

▶ 저는 겨울에 감기 자주 걸려요.

08

↳ [저는 겨우레 감:기 자주 걸려요.]

= I often catch colds in the winter.

▶ 저희 집 강아지 건강이 너무 걱정돼요.

09

↳ [저히 집 강아지 건:강이 너무 걱쩡돼요.]

= I'm so worried about our puppy's health.

▶ 거기 있는 그거 고장 났어요.

10

↳ [거기 인는 그거 고:장 나써요.]

= That thing over there is broken.

Lesson 2

What Are the Differences Between N and ㄴ, and D and ㄷ?

⏵ Listen to the pronunciation of a native speaker and choose the consonant
01 that correctly corresponds with the first sound.

ㅜ구

ⓐ ㄴ ⓑ ㄷ

The word pronounced by the native speaker is "누구 (= who)". Did you
happen to choose ㄷ instead of ㄴ? Or did you choose ㄴ here, but other times
have noticed that words with ㄴ sometimes sound like the English *d* or the
Korean ㄷ?

In this lesson, we will learn and practice how to pronounce ㄴ and ㄷ. After
this lesson, you will no longer confuse the ㄴ and ㄷ sounds.

First, let's compare the English *n* sound with the Korean ㄴ sound.

Both are pronounced by exhaling air through both the mouth and the nose.
However, **the amount of air released from the nose when pronouncing ㄴ is
far less than when pronouncing *n*.** When pronouncing ㄴ, the sound is short.
What do we mean by that? It means **that when you pronounce ㄴ, you place**

your tongue against the roof of your mouth for a shorter amount of time than when you pronounce *n*. To pronounce ㄴ, you can tap your tongue to the roof of your mouth. As you release your tongue, pronounce the vowel following ㄴ.

⊙ **We will try pronouncing the ㄴ in "나 (= I)" once like *n*, and once correctly, so**
02 **listen and compare.**

ⓐ 나   ⓑ 나

What do you think? Are you able to tell the difference?

● **This time, try pronouncing it yourself.**

나 I   너 you   네 yes

⊙ **Listen to the native speaker's pronunciation and check if you pronounced it**
03 **correctly.**

If it seems a little different, try changing the position of your tongue slightly. When pronouncing both *n* and ㄴ, the tip of your tongue is located close to your upper teeth. However, there is a slight difference in where it is located. **When you pronounce *n*, the tip of your tongue touches the gums behind your upper teeth. When you pronounce ㄴ, the inner part of your tongue touches your gums.** When some people pronounce ㄴ you might see the tip of their tongue between their upper and lower teeth. This is because the tip of their tongue touches their upper teeth, rather than the gums behind their upper teeth.

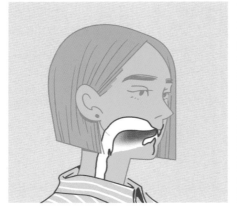

Position of the tongue when pronouncing *n*

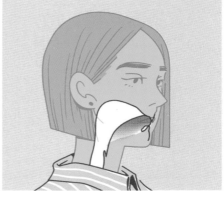

Position of the tongue when pronouncing ㄴ

- Shall we try once more, paying attention to the position of the tongue? You can pronounce the words by positioning your tongue as shown in the picture above and opening your mouth straight from that position to pronounce the vowel.

너 I   너 you   네 yes

How did you do? Has your pronunciation gotten closer to the native speaker's?

The same technique applies when you pronounce ㄴ as the final consonant. The inner part of your tongue, slightly behind the tip, touches your gums or upper teeth, and the tip of your tongue should be slightly visible between your upper and lower teeth.

An important point when pronouncing ㄴ as the final consonant is that **you should not make any movement or sound with your vocal cords after you release your tongue from the roof of your mouth.**

Let's practice the pronunciation of ㄴ as the first sound of a syllable and as the last sound of syllable. Listen to the native speaker's pronunciation first, and then practice to the beat.

· 아 나 안 · 이 니 인

· 애 내 앤 · 어 너 언

· 오 노 온 · 우 누 운

Now do you understand the difference between the sound of ㄴ in Korean and the sound of *n* in English?

This time, let's practice with a few commonly used words and expressions that contain ㄴ. To begin with, we'll practice words where ㄴ is the first sound. The native speaker will read at a normal speed. Practice at the same pace as the native speaker so that the ㄴ sound is not prolonged.

누구 who

내일 tomorrow

나라 country

나이프 knife

노트 note; notebook

노래 song

농구 basketball

누나 older sister (used by men)

나누기 division (÷)

남녀노소 men and women of all ages

▶ 06 This time, let's practice some words where the ㄴ sound is at both the beginning and end of a syllable. Listen and repeat.

눈 eye

난 as for me (short for 나는)

넌 as for you (short for 너는)

논 rice paddy

-는 topic marking particle

▶ 07 Now, listen to the expression below containing 누구 (= who) that you heard at the beginning of the lesson.

누구세요? Who are you?

Do you know why 누구 sounded like 두구? In Korean, ㄴ is short and has a weak nasal sound. Because of this, it sometimes sounds like *d*/ㄷ, a sound in which the vocal cords are engaged but air does not come out of the nose.

If that is the case, are the pronunciations of *d* and ㄷ similar?

No. There is one very big difference between ㄷ and *d*. The difference is that *d* is pronounced by engaging the vocal cords, but in most cases ㄷ is not. Because the vocal cords are not engaged, ㄷ is actually more similar to the English *t*. However, <u>you exhale less air pronouncing ㄷ than you do when pronouncing *t*.</u> If you exhale too much air, it can sound like ㅌ.

You learned the difference between ㄷ and ㅌ in Chapter 1 Lesson 2, right? When the vowel ㅡ is attached and pronounced as 드 and 트, 드 sounds lower than 트 and less air is exhaled.

(▶) Shall we practice first pronouncing ㅌ and then changing it to 드?
08

트 트 드 드

트 트 드 드

트 드

트 드

드 드

When pronouncing *d*, the tip of your tongue touches your gums behind your upper teeth. Therefore, when viewed from the front, your tongue is not visible. However, **when pronouncing ㄷ, like when pronouncing ㄴ, you might see the tip of some people's tongue between their upper and lower teeth.**

● **Let's practice one more time, paying attention to the position of the tongue.**

You can simply think of it as the tongue positions of *n* and *d* being almost the same, and the tongue positions of ㄴ and ㄷ being almost the same.

● **Shall we try practicing while paying attention to the position of the tongue?**

다 더 데 디

▶ **Check the native speaker's pronunciation.**
09

▶ **Now, let's practice our pronunciation with words that contain ㄷ. Let's start with words with ㄷ at the beginning of the word. Listen and repeat the native speaker's pronunciation.**
10

다음 next, the following   두유 soy milk

다리미 iron   도시 city

드라마 drama   두바이 Dubai

대학교 university, college   돼지 pig

The following words have ㄷ in the middle, rather than at the beginning of the word. The ㄷ sound is not usually made by engaging the vocal cords like with *t*, but when you pronounce a ㄷ sound that is located between two vowels, or between a nasal consonant and a vowel, the vocal cords are sometimes engaged. So the ㄷ sound in the words or expressions below may feel a little bit different from the ㄷ sound we practiced above. However, depending on the person and the speed at which they are speaking, sometimes the vocal cords are engaged and sometimes they are not. There is no need to intentionally engage them in order to make a sound.

▶ It would be better to focus more on the proper pronunciation of ㄷ and the
11 vowel sounds that we practiced earlier.

반드시 certainly; at any cost

운동 exercise

자동 automatic

사람들 people

감동받았어요. [감:동바다써요.] I am touched.

기대돼요. I look forward to it.

힘들어요. [힘드러요.] It is hard.

● Lastly, we will practice with ㄴ and ㄷ together.

나 ㅣ 다 all

네 yes 데 place

내기 bet 대기 waiting, stand-by

▶ **Check the native speaker's pronunciation and practice again.**
12

▶ **Finally, let's practice with words that include both ㄴ and ㄷ in one word!**
13

농담 joke

덧니 [던니] snaggletooth

냉동실 freezer compartment

당뇨 diabetes

돈 money

네덜란드 Netherlands

나도. Me, too. (casual speech)

단단해요. It is firm.

Quiz Time!

▶ Listen to the following and check which sound is said more than the other.

Ex1. ○ ● ● ● ●
◀» 디 니 니 니 니   ☑ⓐ니 ⓑ디

Q1. ⓐ 나 ⓑ 다

Q2. ⓐ 너 ⓑ 더

Q3. ⓐ 노 ⓑ 도

Q4. ⓐ 네 ⓑ 데

▶ Listen to the word and choose the correct consonant.

Q5.

Q6.

Q7.
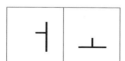

Q8.

Q9.

Let's practice with sentences!

▶ Now, let's practice using the words we have learned in sentences.

Q10. 누나랑 농구 하다가 덧니를 다쳤어요.

    ↳ [누:나랑 농구 하다가 던니를 다처써요.]

    = I injured my snaggletooth while I was playing basketball with my older sister.

Q11. 남대문 시장에서 나비 그림 그려진 노트 샀어요.

    ↳ [남대문 시:장에서 나비 그:림 그:려진 노트 사써요.]

    = I bought a notebook with a butterfly on it at Namdaemun Market.

Q12. 두유는 냉동실 말고 냉장실에 넣으세요.

    ↳ [두유는 냉:동실 말고 냉:장시레 너:으세요.]

    = Put the soy milk in the fridge, not the freezer.

Q13. 남녀노소 누구나 좋아할 만한 노래예요.

    ↳ [남녀노소 누구나 조:아할 만한 노래예요.]

    = It's a song that everyone, young and old, will love.

Q14. 두바이에 다녀온 친구가 다리미를 선물해 줘서 감동받았어요.

    ↳ [두바이에 다녀온 친구가 다리미를 선:물해 줘서 감:동바다써요.]

    = A friend who went to Dubai gave me an iron as a gift, and I was so moved.

Answers

Q1. ⓐ (나나나나다)

Q2. ⓑ (너더더더더)

Q3. ⓑ (노노도도도)

Q4. ⓐ (네네네데데)

Q5. ㄴ (나비 = butterfly)

Q6. ㄷ (다양한 = various; different)

Q7. ㄴ, ㄷ (너도 = you, too)

Q8. ㄷ, ㄷ (대답 = answer, reply)

Q9. ㄴ, ㄷ (남대문 = Namdaemun,
the South Gate)

Lesson 3

What Are the Differences Between M and ㅁ, and B and ㅂ?

▶ **Listen to the native speaker's pronunciation.**
01

Is the word pronounced by the native speaker 매워요 or 배워요?

매워요. It is spicy.   배워요. I learn.

The native speaker said 매워요. Did you happen to hear 배워요? Why do Koreans sound like they are saying ㅂ when they pronounce ㅁ? In this lesson, you will find out, and you will also be able to check whether or not you have been pronouncing ㅁ and ㅂ properly.

First, let's compare the sound of *m* and ㅁ.

▶ **Listen to the native speaker's pronunciation**
02

Moo 무 [무ː] radish

What do you think? Can you tell the difference?

▶ **This time, we will try pronouncing the ㅁ in the word 무게 once like an**
03 **English *m* and once properly, so listen and compare.**

ⓐ 무게   ⓑ 무게

What do you think? Can you tell the difference between the first □ sound and the second □ sound?

When you first learned the Korean consonant □, you probably thought that it was almost the same as *m*. Yes, it is very similar. But it is not exactly the same. That is why □ may have sounded like ㅂ to you. Once you know the difference, you will not confuse □ and ㅂ when listening, and you will be able to pronounce both more like a native speaker when speaking.

Both *m* and □ are sounds made by releasing air from the nose as well as from the mouth. However, **the □ sound is much less nasal than the *m* sound. (Some say that □ can be pronounced more accurately with your nose blocked.) The □ sound is also a little bit shorter.**

The sound is shorter... What does that mean?

Whether the first sound of a syllable is □ or *m*, you pronounce it by closing your mouth and then opening it. However, **when you pronounce *m*, you start making a sound before you open your mouth, and when you pronounce □, you make the sound as you open your mouth.** Therefore, the pronunciation of "moo" in English can sound like [음무] to Korean speakers, not [무ː].

Another difference is that **when you pronounce □, you do not press your lips together as much as when you pronounce *m*.** Think of how you close your mouth when you are not saying anything. When you pronounce □, you press your lips together with just that amount of strength and then open them.

Let's practice the pronunciation by adding various vowels to ㅁ.

▶ **First, listen to the pronunciation of a native speaker.**

05

미 매 마 머 모 무

● **Now, try reading it yourself.**

Shall we look at ㅁ as the final consonant sound this time? It is the same. ㅁ is pronounced much shorter when it is the last sound of a word than when the English *m* is the last sound. After closing your mouth, you should not engage your vocal cords at all. Let's practice pronouncing ㅁ as both the first sound of a syllable and as the last sound of a syllable.

▶ **Listen to the native speaker's pronunciation first, then practice to the beat.**
06

- 아　마　암　· 이　미　임
- 애　매　앰　· 어　머　엄
- 오　모　옴　· 우　무　움

Now do you understand the difference between the sound of the Korean ㅁ and the sound of the English *m*?

This time, let's practice with some commonly used words and expressions that contain ㅁ.

▶ **First, let's look at words that have ㅁ as the first sound of the syllable. The**
07 **native speaker will read at normal speed. Practice at the pace of the native speaker so that the ㅁ sound is not prolonged.**

뭐 what

머리 head; hair; brain

문제 problem; question

메모 memo

목요일 [모교일] Thursday

물 water

명함 business card

며칠 a few days; what date

멀미 motion sickness; travel sickness

미안해. I'm sorry.

▶ **08** This time, the ㅁ sound is at both the beginning and the end of the syllable. Again, the native speaker will read at a normal speed. Practice at the pace of the native speaker.

몸 body

몸매 body shape

몸무게 weight

맘 mind, heart, feeling (short for 마음)

맘껏 as much as one likes (short for 마음껏)

맘마미아! Mamma Mia!

▶ **09** Now, listen to "매워요" one more time.

매워요. It is spicy.

Do you hear it differently now, compared to how it sounded at the beginning of the lesson?

If you happen to still hear it as "배워요", let's move on to looking at the pronunciation of ㅂ in more detail.

ㅂ is also different from the English *b* sound. The English *b* is a sound made by engaging the vocal cords, but ㅂ is not. In fact, ㅂ is actually more similar to the English *p* sound because it does not engage the vocal cords. You also exhale less air when you pronounce ㅂ than when you pronounce *b*. Otherwise, ㅂ can sound like ㅍ.

You learned the difference between ㅂ and ㅍ in Chapter 1 Lesson 3, right? When the vowel ㅡ is added and ㅂ and ㅍ are pronounced as 브 and 프, 브 sounds lower than 프 and less air is exhaled.

▶ **Shall we first practice by pronouncing 프 and then changing it into 브?**

10

프 프 브 브

프 프 브 브

프 브

프 브

브 브

Did you practice many times?

Good. Remember the feeling when you pronounced the final 브, and now let's practice combining other vowels with ㅂ.

비 rain　　ㅃ belly, stomach; boat; pear　　바보 fool

▶ **First, listen to the native speaker's pronunciation.**
11

Just like when pronouncing ㅁ, when you pronounce ㅂ, you pronounce the vowel combined with ㅂ by lightly closing your mouth and then quickly opening it.

● **Shall we try pronouncing it?**

▶ **Let's practice with other words that contain ㅂ.**
12

바람 wind

배우 actor/actress

바구니 basket

비누 soap

반대 opposition

번개 lightning

아버지 father

부분 part

붐벼요. It is crowded.

부드러워요. It is soft.

◉ This time, let's practice by comparing ㅂ with ㅁ. Listen and repeat the native
13 speaker's pronunciation.

ㅂ│ rain   ㅁ│ mi (musical note)

ㅐㅐ belly, stomach; boat; pear   ㅁㅐ rod; every; hawk

ㅂㅏㅂㅗ fool   ㅁㅏㅁㅗ abrasion

By any chance, did you happen to hear a difference in pronunciation between
the first ㅂ and the second ㅂ in 바보?

Although we said earlier that you do not engage your vocal cords when
pronouncing ㅂ, when ㅂ falls between two vowels, or between a nasal
sound and a vowel, sometimes you engage your vocal cords to pronounce it.
However, whether or not ㅂ is voiced depends on the person and the speed at
which they are speaking, so there is no need to be too concerned.

Good. Finally, let's practice with words that contain both ㅁ and ㅂ.

◉ Listen carefully to the native speaker and read along at the same speed.
14

방문 visit

비밀 secret

부모님 parents

분명히 clearly

별명 nickname

금방 a short time ago; immediately, quickly

불만 dissatisfaction

반말 informal/casual language

비밀번호 password

물어보세요. [무러보세요.] Ask (someone).

Quiz Time!

▶ Listen to the audio and select which of the two words was pronounced.

Q1. ⓐ 문 ⓑ 분   Q2. ⓐ 말 ⓑ 발

Q3. ⓐ 목 ⓑ 복   Q4. ⓐ 밑 ⓑ 빚

Q5. ⓐ 미용 ⓑ 비용   Q6. ⓐ 모자 ⓑ 보자

Did you check your answers? Click on the next track to listen to the pronunciation and follow along.

문 door

말 speech; words; language

목 neck; throat

밑 bottom

미용 beauty care; hairdressing

모자 hat

분 minute

발 foot

복 luck; fortune

빚 debt; loan

비용 cost; expense

보자. Let's see/meet.

▶ Listen to the words and write which consonant, either ㅁ or ㅂ, goes in the blank.

Q8.

ㅓ	지

Q9.

ㅏ	른

Q10.

굴	난	두

Q11.

꾼	ㅕ

Q12.

ㅣ	ㅣ	지	마

Let's practice with sentences!

▶ **Q13** 부모님한테 반말해요?

= You use informal language with your parents?

▶ **Q14** 몸무게를 왜 물어봐요?

↳ [몸무게를 왜: 무러봐요?]

= Why are you asking about my weight?

▶ **Q15** 비밀번호는 제 별명이에요.

= The password is my nickname.

▶ **Q16** 미안해. 목요일에 보자.

↳ [미안해. 모교이레 보자.]

= Sorry. Let's see each other on Thursday.

▶ **Q17** 멀미 때문에 머리가 너무 어지러워요.

↳ [멀미 때무네 머리가 너무 어지러워요.]

= I'm so dizzy because of motion sickness.

Answers

Q1. ⓐ	Q8. ㅁ (먼지 = dust)
Q2. ⓑ	Q9. ㅂ (바른 = straight; upright)
Q3. ⓐ	Q10. ㅁ, ㅁ (물만두 = boiled dumpling)
Q4. ⓑ	Q11. ㅁ, ㅂ (문병 = a visit to a sick person)
Q5. ⓑ	Q12. ㅂ, ㅂ (비비지 마. = Don't rub.)
Q6. ⓐ	

Lesson 4

What Are the Differences Between L, R, and ㄹ?

▶ **Which person pronounced the Korean word 라디오 correctly?**
01
Check the correct answer.

ⓐ (   ) ⓑ (   )

The second person is the one who correctly pronounced ㄹ in Korean.

Shall we check if your pronunciation is like a native speaker?
● **Try to pronounce 라디오.**

라ㅏㄷㅣㅇ오

▶ **Check the native speaker's pronunciation again.**
02

What do you think? Is your pronunciation similar to the native speaker's?

When you pronounce the *r* sound in English, your tongue does not touch the roof of your mouth. However, when you pronounce ㄹ in Korean, the tip of your tongue touches the roof of your mouth.

Chapter 7 – Lesson 4   (231)

The position of the tongue when pronouncing *r*

The position of the tongue when pronouncing ㄹ

Since the tip of your tongue touches the roof of your mouth when pronouncing ㄹ, you might think that ㄹ is similar to the pronunciation of the English *l*. However, the position of your tongue when pronouncing *l* is a little different. **When pronouncing *l*, the tip of your tongue touches the gums behind your upper teeth, or rests between your upper and lower teeth, similar to when you pronounce the sound *th* in English. However, when pronouncing ㄹ, your tongue touches a bit further back inside your mouth.** To pronounce ㄹ, place the tip of your tongue against the gums behind your front teeth, and then bring it a little inwards in your mouth. There will be a spot on the roof of your mouth that suddenly dips. The ㄹ pronunciation is made by lightly flicking your tongue off of this spot.

The position of the tongue when pronouncing *l*

The position of the tongue when pronouncing ㄹ

How To Sound Like A Native Korean Speaker

▶ **03** Now, let's practice with some words that begin with the ㄹ sound. Listen to the native speaker's pronunciation and follow along.

라면 ramyeon   라디오 radio

러시아 Russia   러그 rug

레몬 lemon   리본 ribbon

로그인 login

▶ **04** Next let's practice with some examples where ㄹ comes between two vowels. Listen to the native speaker's pronunciation and follow along.

요리 cooking   수리 repair

나라 country   사람 person

자랑 boast   사랑해요. I love you.

가로등 street lights   그리워요. I miss it.

Let's practice words that have ㄹ at the end. In other words, let's practice the sound that ㄹ makes when used in the final consonant position. When ㄹ is in the final consonant position, your tongue is touching the roof of your mouth, but you do not flick your tongue off of it.

The position of the tongue when pronouncing ㄹ

(▶) Let's listen to the native speaker's pronunciation and follow along.
05

일 one

길 road, street

불 fire

정말 really; fact

보물 treasure

마늘 garlic

팔찌 bracelet

Finally, we will practice examples where two ㄹ sounds come one after the other. These are words and phrases in which ㄹ is used as a final consonant and is then followed by a syllable beginning with another ㄹ. In order to pronounce the two ㄹ in succession, you just need to hold your tongue to the roof of your mouth and then release it into the vowel sound of the second syllable. Easy, right?

06 **Let's listen to the native speaker's pronunciation and follow along.**

빨래 laundry

몰래 secretly

별로 not really, not particularly

벌레 worm; bug

알람 alarm

달력 calendar

몰라요. I don't know.

물론이죠. [물로니죠.] Of course.

놀랐어요. [놀:라써요.] I was surprised.

흘렸어요. [흘려써요.] I spilled.

What do you think? You should not have any problem with the ㄹ sound by now. Are you excited to have mastered the ㄹ sound? Then let's learn a sound we make when we are excited and joyful.

랄랄라

Let's practice one last time with excitement!

Now, let's practice with sentences that contain lots of ㄹ sounds.

First, read the sentences below slowly. Then, listen to the native speaker's pronunciation. Practice and repeat.

07 러그에 라면 흘렸어요.
↳ [러그에 라면 흘려써요.]
= I spilled ramyeon on the rug.

08 알람이 울려서 놀랐어요.
↳ [알라미 울려서 놀:라써요.]
= The alarm rang and surprised me.

09 로그인 비밀번호 몰라요.
= I don't know the login password.

10 정말 유리 씨가 한 요리예요?
= Is this really food that Yuri cooked?

11 라디오에서 마늘 가격이 많이 올랐다고 나왔어요.
↳ [라디오에서 마늘 가겨기 마:니 올랃따고 나와써요.]
= On the radio they said that the price of garlic has risen a lot.

Lesson 5

ㅅ *the Chameleon*

● **Read the word below aloud.**

 sushi

(▶) **Check the native speaker's pronunciation.**

01

Did the ㅅ of the first syllable and the ㅅ of the second syllable sound a little bit different?

When ㅅ is combined with ㅡ, ㅏ, ㅓ, ㅔ, or ㅐ, it is actually pronounced slightly differently than when it is combined with ㅣ or ㅟ. When combined with the vowels ㅣ or ㅟ, ㅅ sounds like the English *sh* rather than *s*, right?

Shall we practice a bit more to get used to it?

First, let's practice with expressions that combine ㅅ with the vowel ㅣ in one syllable. When pronouncing 시, your lips are flat on both sides, just like when pronouncing 이, and the front of your tongue is in contact with your lower gums. Air is exhaled between your palate and your tongue.

▶ **Listen to the native speaker's pronunciation and repeat.**
02

시 poem; o'clock

Shall we practice with some other expressions where 시 is used?

▶ **Listen to the native speaker's pronunciation and follow along.**
03

시험 exam

다시 again

시장 market

점심 lunch

관심 interest; attention

시킬까요? Shall we order it?

싱거워요. It tastes bland.

신청하세요. Apply for it.

● **This time, read the four syllables below out loud.**

샤 셔 쇼 슈

▶ **Check the native speaker's pronunciation.**
04

How To Sound Like A Native Korean Speaker

What do you think? ㅅ sounded like the English sound *sh* this time too, right?
This is because ㅑ, ㅕ, ㅛ, ㅠ are double consonants that begin with ㅣ.

$$ㅑ = ㅣ + ㅏ$$

$$ㅕ = ㅣ + ㅓ$$

$$ㅛ = ㅣ + ㅗ$$

$$ㅠ = ㅣ + ㅜ$$

In other words, 샤 is 시아 pronounced quickly, 셔 is 시어 pronounced quickly, 쇼 is 시오 pronounced quickly, and 슈 is 시우 pronounced quickly. Because of this, ㅅ makes a *sh* sound.

● **Shall we try pronouncing them again?**

▶ **Let's practice with words that include 샤, 셔, 쇼, and 슈.**
05

샤워 shower

샴푸 shampoo

티셔츠 t-shirt

셔틀버스 [셔틀버쓰/셔틀뻐쓰] shuttle bus

마셔요. I drink.

슈크림빵 cream puff

슈렉 Shrek

커피숍 coffee shop

This time, let's practice a word where ㅅ is combined with ㅟ.

● **First, try pronouncing the word below.**

쉬 pee; wee-wee; tinkle

ㅟ is a double vowel that is a quick pronunciation of ㅜ and ㅣ. Even if you add ㅅ here, the shape of the mouth is the same. However, the tip of your tongue is placed on your lower gums like when pronouncing 시.

▶ **Listen to the native speaker's pronunciation and follow along.**

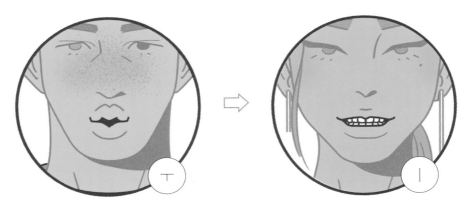

How To Sound Like A Native Korean Speaker

Now, let's practice with words containing 쉬.

▶ **Listen to the native speaker's pronunciation and follow along.**
07

쉰 살 fifty years old

쉿 shush

쉽게 [쉽:께] easily

쉬는 시간 break time

쉬었어요. [쉬어써요.] I had a break.

쉬세요. Get some rest.

This time, let's put the words we have practiced into sentences.

First, try reading them slowly. Then practice reading them again faster and faster.

▶ 쉬는 시간에는 좀 쉬세요.
08
↳ [쉬:는 시가네는 좀 쉬:세요.]

= Rest during the break time.

▶ 커피숍에서 좀 쉬었어요.
09
↳ [커피쇼베서 좀 쉬어써요.]

= I took a break at the cafe.

▶ 슈렉처럼 생긴 슈크림빵 봤어요?

10
   ↳ [슈렉처럼 생긴 슈크림빵 봐써요?]

= Did you see the cream puff that looks like Shrek?

▶ 쉿! 지금 시험 시작했어요.

11
   ↳ [쉳! 지금 시험 시:자캐써요.]

= Shh! The test has started now.

▶ 관심 있으시면 신청하세요.

12
   ↳ [관심 이쓰시면 신청하세요.]

= Please apply if you're interested.

Lesson 6

What Is The Difference Between J and ㅈ?

(▶) Try pronouncing 젤리. Next, listen to the two people pronounce
01 젤리. Which person correctly pronounced the ㅈ sound?

젤리  jelly ⓐ (　　) ⓑ (　　)

The second person is the one who correctly pronounced ㅈ. The first person's pronunciation sounds more like 쥍리 than 젤리 to a native Korean speaker's ears. Why might that be? It is because ㅈ was pronounced like the English "j[dʒ]". In this lesson, we will find out exactly what the difference is in pronunciation between j and ㅈ, and how to pronounce ㅈ correctly!

The sounds j and ㅈ sound similar at first, but once you learn the difference between them, you realize the difference is quite large.

First, the way they are spoken is different. The sound j is pronounced using the vocal cords, but ㅈ is not. If your vocal cords engage when you pronounce ㅈ, it is probably because of the vowel attached to ㅈ. ㅈ is rather similar to the sound ch because the vocal cords are not engaged. However, you exhale less air when pronouncing ㅈ than you do when pronouncing ch. If you exhale too much air, ㅈ will sound like ㅊ.

In Chapter 1 Lesson 5, you learned the difference between the sounds ㅈ and ㅊ, right? When the vowel ㅡ is added and they are pronounced as 즈 and 츠, 즈 sounds lower than 츠 and less air is exhaled.

(▶) Let's practice pronouncing ㅊ and then changing it to ㅈ first.

02

ㅊ ㅊ ㅈ ㅈ

ㅊ ㅊ ㅈ ㅈ

ㅊ ㅈ

ㅊ ㅈ

ㅈ ㅈ

● **Try practicing by repeating it.**

Did you find the ㅈ sound?

Is it still difficult to pronounce ㅈ like a native speaker? If so, check the shape of your mouth. When pronouncing *ch* or *j*, you bring your lips together and push them out in a round shape. However, that is not the case with ㅈ. Instead, ㅈ is pronounced by comfortably opening your mouth and directly pronouncing the vowel.

The shape of the mouth when pronouncing *ch* or *j*   The shape of the mouth when pronouncing ㅈ

You may wonder, is mouth shape really that important? Yes, it is! If you pronounce ㅈ with the same mouth shape as *ch* or *j*, it can sound like 주

rather than 즈. At the beginning of the lesson, 젤리 sounded like 쳴리—that was due to mouth shape!

● Try pronouncing 즈 again, paying attention to the shape of your mouth.

즈

● Shall we practice by combining ㅈ with ㅏ as well? Be careful not to gather your lips into a rounded shape, then relax and pronounce ㅏ at almost the same time as ㅈ.

자 ruler

▶ Now, listen to the native speaker's pronunciation of 자.
03

What do you think? Is there still a difference between your pronunciation and the native speaker's pronunciation? If so, this time try checking the position of your tongue. When pronouncing *ch* or *j*, the tip of your tongue touches the gums behind your upper teeth, but when pronouncing ㅈ, the tip of your tongue is behind your lower teeth as shown in the picture below.

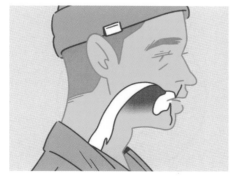

The position of the tongue
when pronouncing *ch* or *j*

The position of the tongue
when pronouncing ㅈ

● Let's practice again, paying attention to the position of the tongue.

자

Try to apply the three points we learned above.

(1) Exhale less air than when pronouncing *ch*.

(2) Start with your mouth relaxed and slightly open.

(3) Place the tip of your tongue behind your lower teeth, and place the middle
section of your tongue on the roof of your mouth.

Let's practice by combining ㅈ with the vowels ㅏ, ㅓ, ㅣ, and ㅐ. Using the
video, listen to the native speaker's pronunciation and repeat. Pay attention
to the shape of their mouth.

04

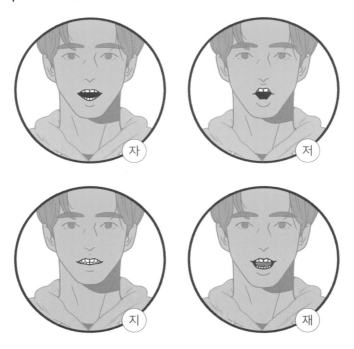

자
저
지
재

What do you think? Has your pronunciation gotten closer to the native speaker's?

How To Sound Like A Native Korean Speaker

(▶) Now, let's practice with some other vowels. Using the video, listen to the
05 native speaker's pronunciation and repeat. Pay attention to the shape of their
mouth this time as well.

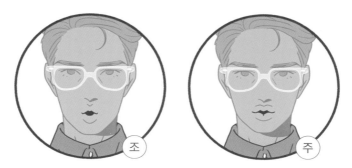

(●) Lastly, let's practice 죄, which is used often when saying, "죄송합니다." In
order to pronounce 조 + 에, you must first round your lips. However, the ㅗ
should be pronounced as a very short sound. As soon as the ㅗ sound is
made, immediately make the 에 mouth shape and say 에.

(▶) Practice again while watching the video.
06

Now, have you gotten used to the ㅈ sound?

When you first learn a language, connecting the new sounds that you
are learning to similar sounds in your native language helps you with
remembering. However, it can also interfere with being able to pronounce

things like a native speaker. From now on, let's practice the ㅈ sound until we completely forget the *j* sound. Listen carefully to the native speaker's pronunciation and read along!

● **Let's practice with some words and short phrases first.**

▶ 07

자리 seat   자매 sisters

장마 rainy season   잠 sleep

잔소리 nagging

▶ 08

저기요. Excuse me.   저도요. Me too.

이 정도 this much   점수 [점쑤/점수] score

전기 electricity

▶ 09

제일 first; most   재미있어요. [재미이써요.] It is fun/interesting.

제발. Please.   세제 detergent

▶ 10

지하 basement   아직 yet; still

진해요. It is thick.   지루해요. It is boring.

반지 ring

▶ **11** 조각 piece　　　　조용해요. It is quiet.

조심하세요. Be careful.　　종이 paper

만족해요. [만조캐요.] I am satisfied.

▶ **12** 주소 address　　　　매주 every week

주머니 pocket　　　　주문할게요. [주:문할께요.] I will order it.

중요해요. It is important.

▶ **13** 죄 sin　　　　　　범죄 crime

죄송합니다. [죄:송함니다.] I am sorry.

This time, the words below include ㅈ more than once.

▶ **14** **Listen to the native speaker's pronunciation and follow along.**

자주 often　　　　잠자리 dragonfly

점점 gradually　　　주제 subject, topic

자전거 bicycle　　　주장 argument, claim

진주 pearl　　　　가전제품 home appliances

Now, let's practice by inserting the words we practiced earlier into sentences.

Read them to yourself first, then check the native speaker's pronunciation.
Then, read them again.

▶ 저기요. 여기 자리 있어요?
15
↳ [저기요. 여기 자리 이써요?]

= Excuse me. Is this seat available?

▶ 진주야, 진주 갈 때 진주 반지 끼고 가.
16
= Jinjoo, when you go to Jinju, wear a pearl ring.

▶ 저희 반에서 제 점수가 제일 높아요. 정말이에요.
17
↳ [저히 바네서 제 점수가 제:일 노파요. 정:마리에요.]

= In our class, my score is the highest. Really.

▶ 조용히 좀 해. 잠 좀 자자.
18
= Be quiet. Let's sleep.

▶ 자전거랑 가전제품 주문할게요.
19
↳ [자전거랑 가전제품 주:문할께요.]

= I'll order bikes and appliances.

Real Experiences by Korean Learners

This anecdote shared by Kampy, Germany

동이에요 동.

...똥.

When I was a teacher, I once couldn't pronounce a student's name because it had ㄷ
in the beginning. The German *d* sounds more like ㄸ, and I think I was saying a bad word
when I pronounced it with ㄸ because the other students always laughed when I said his name.
I don't remember the name exactly, maybe something with Dong in it.

CHAPTER 8.

Not Quite English

Lesson 1

Sit on the Bench, Not on My Benz.

▶ **Listen to the audio and guess what the word is.**
01

What do you think? Do you know what the word is?

The word is 마트 (mart). In Korea, large supermarkets such as Walmart and Costco are called 마트, so it is a word that is heard often in everyday life. It sounds a lot different from the English word "mart" though, right?

▶ **Listen and compare the English word "mart" with the Korean word 마트.**
02

mart [mɑːrt]   마트 [마ㅌ]

If you thought, "Why should I pronounce 'mart' as 마트?" or, "Since this is an English word, I don't need to learn how to pronounce it", that would be a mistake. This is because the pronunciation of loanwords in Korean is surprisingly different from how the original word is pronounced, and it is often impossible to communicate properly unless you can pronounce it in the Korean way.

In this chapter, you will learn how to pronounce loanwords like native Korean speakers! * Loanword: A word that comes from a foreign language but is used like a Korean word

One of the differences between Korean and English is that consonants in

Korean cannot be pronounced alone. So if a loanword in English ends in a consonant, you have to add a vowel to say it in Korean.

For example, in "mart", the "t" can be pronounced aloud, but if you write it in Korean as 마ㅌ, ㅌ cannot be read aloud. That is why you must add the ㅡ vowel in order to make it 마트.

There are so many loanwords created by adding the ㅡ vowel to the final consonant. Let's practice pronouncing words that are used often in everyday life.

Listen and follow along.

03

mask [mæsk]	마스크
tube [tuːb]	튜브
card [kɑːrd]	카드
graph [græf]	그래프
hint [hɪnt]	힌트
percent [pərsent]	퍼센트
skate [skeɪt]	스케이트
zigzag [zɪgzæg]	지그재그

But the problem is, not all loanwords end with ㅡ. There are also some words where ㅣ is used instead of ㅡ. For example, if you were to write "bench" in Korean, how would it change?

▶ If you add ㅡ to 벤ㅊ, it becomes 벤츠, but bench is 벤치, not 벤츠 in Korean.

04

bench [bentʃ]   벤치|

Like "bench", if a word ends with the [tʃ] sound or the [ʒ], [dʒ], or [ʃ] sounds, ㅣ is added instead of ㅡ.

▶ Shall we see what other words there are like this?

05

image [ɪmɪdʒ]	이미지
page [peɪdʒ]	페이지
sponge [spʌndʒ]	스펀지
vintage [vɪntɪdʒ]	빈티지
punch [pʌntʃ]	펀치
massage [məsɑːʒ]	마사지 [마싸지]
flash [flæʃ]	플래시

In the case of a word like "flash", since there is no *f* sound in Korean, the pronunciation becomes something like "plash".

▶ **Let's look at some similar words.**

06

fan [fæn]	팬
fashion [fæʃn]	패션
fork [fɔːrk]	포크
file [faɪl]	파일
France [fræns]	프랑스 [프랑쓰]

▶ **Like *f*, what other sounds are not found in Korean? How about the *v* sound? Because there is no *v* sound in Korean, *v* changes to ㅂ. The *b* sound in English changes to ㅂ as well.**

07

version [vɜːrʒn]	버전
vitamin [vaɪtəmɪn]	비타민
van [væn]	밴
virus [vaɪrəs]	바이러스 [바이러쓰]
violin [vaɪəlɪn]	바이올린

There's no *r* sound in Korean either, right? So the letters *l* and *r* are both changed to ㄹ in Korean. As you learned in a previous chapter, ㄹ is different from both *l* and *r*.

▶ **Let's listen and follow along with the words below.**
08

radio [reɪdioʊ]	라디오
robot [roʊbɑːt]	로봇
rap [ræp]	랩
replay [riːpleɪ]	리플레이
recipe [resəpi]	레시피
rumor [ruːmər]	루머

▶ **Lastly, shall we take a look at how the *wh* sound is different in Korean?**
09

white [waɪt]　화이트

When a word starting with *wh* is used like a Korean word, *wh* becomes ㅎ. "White" and 화이트 are completely different, right?

▶ **There is one more case in which *wh* becomes ㅎ.**
10

wheelchair [wiːltʃer] 휠체어

Great! Now you have a grasp of what "Korean" pronunciation is. Let's practice with some sentences.

Listen carefully to the audio and try following along.

▶ **마트**에 가서 **스펀지** 사 올게요.
11   ↳ [마트에 가서 스펀지 사 올께요.]
= I will go to the supermarket and buy a sponge.

▶ 이 **파일**은 최신 **버전**이에요?
12   ↳ [이 파이른 최:신 버저니에요?]
= Is this file the newest version?

▶ **빈티지** 가게에서 산 **라디오**예요.
13   = It's a radio I bought at a vintage shop.

▶ 그 **멤버**는 **랩**을 잘해서 **팬**이 많아요.
14   ↳ [그 멤버는 래블 잘해서 패니 마:나요.]
= That member raps well, so he/she has a lot of fans.

▶ **프랑스**에서 사 온 **포크**예요.
15   ↳ [프랑쓰에서 사 온 포크예요.]
= It's a fork I bought in France.

▶ 그 **이미지**는 몇 **페이지**에 있어요?
16   ↳ [그 이미지는 면 페이지에 이써요?]
= What page is that image on?

Lesson 2

Why English Is Pronounced Differently in Korean

● **Read the following word aloud.**

(▶) **Shall we listen to the Korean pronunciation this time?**

01

"핫도그 (hot dog)" is an English word, but when it is used in Korean, Koreans pronounce it according to Korean pronunciation rules. So hot dog is pronounced [핟또그]. Yes, this is the rule you learned in Chapter 5 Lesson 1! As the rule states, "ㄱ, ㄷ, ㅂ, ㅅ, or ㅈ connected to the final consonant ㄱ, ㄷ, or ㅂ is pronounced as a voiced consonant." Therefore, if ㅅ is used as a base, it sounds like [ㄷ].

Isn't it fun to apply Korean pronunciation rules to English words?

● **Now, try reading this word aloud.**

 nickname

How did you pronounce it? Let's listen to the Korean pronunciation.
02

How was it? It was pronounced like [닝네임], right? That is because of the rule we learned in Chapter 5 Lesson 2. The rule is that when the final consonant ㄱ is followed by ㄴ or ㅁ, it is pronounced as [ㅇ].

The final consonant ㄱ in the words below is pronounced like [ㅇ] as well.
03

빅뉴스 [빙뉴쓰] big news

북마크 [붕마크] bookmark

Shall we take a look at some more loanwords to which the rule we learned in Chapter 5 Lesson 3 applies? Let's take the name Henry. When Henry is written in Korean, it becomes 헨리. How do Koreans pronounce 헨리?

헨리

Take a listen.
04

That is right. Koreans often pronounce Henry as [헬리].

헨리 [헬리]

"When ㄴ meets ㄹ, it is pronounced like [ㄹ]!"

Do you remember? Then how is the country name "핀란드 (Finland)" pronounced?

핀란드

▶ **Shall we give it a listen?**

05

That is right. Koreans pronounce "핀란드 (Finland)" as [필란드].

핀란드 [필란드]

The phenomenon where ㄴ is pronounced like [ㄹ] is often seen in loanwords in Korean.

● **Try pronouncing the words below.**

온라인 online

다운로드 download

원룸 studio apartment (lit. one room)

▶ **Let's listen to the pronunciation of native Korean speakers this time.**

06

Did you have fun applying Korean pronunciation rules to English words?

● **Finally, let's try pronouncing the words we learned above one more time!**

핫도그 [핟또그]   닉네임 [닝네임]   빅뉴스 [빙뉴쓰]

북마크 [붕마크]   헨리 [헬리]   핀란드 [필란드]

온라인 [올라인]   다운로드 [다울로드]   원룸 [월룸]

Shall we practice with sentences as well?

Listen carefully to the audio and try following along.

07 저희는 서로 **닉네임**으로 불러요.
= We call each other by nicknames.

08 들어 보세요. **빅뉴스**예요, **빅뉴스**!
= Listen to this. It's big news, big news!

09 **헨리** 씨, 이 파일 **다운로드** 받았어요?
= Henry, did you download this file?

10 **핀란드**로 여행 갔다 왔어요.
= I went on vacation to Finland.

11 저는 **원룸**에 살아요.
= I live in a one-room (studio apartment).

Lesson 3

Native Korean Speakers vs. The Dictionary

(▶) Do you know what "chocolate" is in Korean? Listen to ⓐ and ⓑ and guess
01   which one is correct.

(ⓐ) vs (ⓑ)

In example ⓐ, chocolate was pronounced 초콜렛, and in ⓑ, it was
pronounced 초콜릿.

● Shall we look it up in a dictionary?

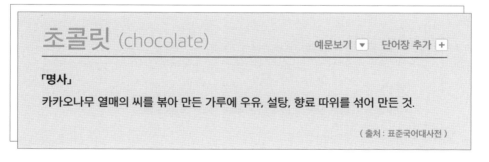

초콜릿 (chocolate)   예문보기 ▼   단어장 추가 +

「명사」
카카오나무 열매의 씨를 볶아 만든 가루에 우유, 설탕, 향료 따위를 섞어 만든 것.

(출처 : 표준국어대사전)

That is right. Chocolate is 초콜릿 in Korean. But have you ever heard how
Koreans pronounce it in real life? You may have heard it pronounced as 초콜렛
more often than 초콜릿.

In reality, people often do not pronounce loanwords exactly as they are listed
in the dictionary.

The reason for this is that when Koreans start to use a word from another language, they immediately write and use it in Hangeul. Later, when the word becomes very commonly used and becomes an official loanword added to the dictionary, it is written using the official loanword rules. In some cases, the spelling that people originally used follows the official loanword pronunciation rules, but in other cases, the two spellings are different.

Here is another example of a loanword with two different pronunciations.

Listen to the audio of the two different ways to say "barbecue".

02

(a) vs (b)

Which pronunciation is more familiar? Is neither familiar?

● **Let's see what is in the dictionary.**

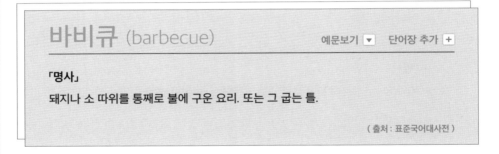

바비큐 (barbecue)   예문보기 ▼   단어장 추가 +

「명사」
돼지나 소 따위를 통째로 불에 구운 요리. 또는 그 굽는 틀.

(출처 : 표준국어대사전)

It says 바비큐, right? However, when Koreans speak to each other in daily life, most people pronounce it as 바베큐.

It is your choice. You can choose to pronounce it as it appears in the dictionary, or to say it in the way that the majority of people pronounce it.

Let's practice both the dictionary pronunciation and the common conversational pronunciations of both words.

초콜릿

초콜렛

바비큐

바베큐

However, of course, if you need to choose the correct spelling on a test, you should choose 초콜릿 and 바비큐. So, if you are preparing for a Korean language test or need to prepare a formal writing excerpt, please memorize the version found in the dictionary.

▶ 04 Let's take a look at some more words that are frequently pronounced differently from how they are found in the dictionary.

	Dictionary	Commonly Used
message	메시지 [메씨지]	메세지 [메쎄지]
sausage	소시지 [쏘시지]	소세지 [쏘세지]
accessory	액세서리 [액쎄서리]	악세사리 [악쎄사리]

As you can see from the difference between the spelling and the pronunciation of these words, the pronunciation uses ㅆ and is closer to the original English pronunciation. However, in writing it is written with just ㅅ. Take this into consideration.

▶ **Shall we look at a few more?**
05

	Dictionary	Commonly Used
Valentine's Day	밸런타인데이	발렌타인데이
encore	앙코르	앵콜
cake	케이크	케익

Quiz Time!

▶ Listen to the audio and choose the correct Korean pronunciation.

Q1. mask ⓐ ⓑ ⓒ   Q2. card ⓐ ⓑ ⓒ

Q3. graph ⓐ ⓑ ⓒ   Q4. skate ⓐ ⓑ ⓒ

Q5. image ⓐ ⓑ ⓒ   Q6. sponge ⓐ ⓑ ⓒ

Q7. massage ⓐ ⓑ ⓒ   Q8. fork ⓐ ⓑ ⓒ

Q9. version ⓐ ⓑ ⓒ   Q10. white ⓐ ⓑ ⓒ

▶ Listen to the audio and choose the most natural pronunciation.

Q11. 핀란드 ⓐ ⓑ ⓒ   Q12. 온라인 ⓐ ⓑ ⓒ

Q13. 닉네임 ⓐ ⓑ ⓒ   Q14. 핫도그 ⓐ ⓑ ⓒ

Q15. 빅뉴스 ⓐ ⓑ ⓒ

▶ Listen to the two pronunciations, and write "D" for the pronunciation as it is written in the dictionary, and "R" for the pronunciation that is used in real-life conversations.

Q16. ⓐ (   ) ⓑ (   )   Q17. ⓐ (   ) ⓑ (   )

Q18. ⓐ (   ) ⓑ (   )   Q19. ⓐ (   ) ⓑ (   )

Q20. ⓐ (   ) ⓑ (   )

Answers

Q1. ⓑ	Q8. ⓑ	Q15. ⓒ
Q2. ⓒ	Q9. ⓒ	Q16. ⓐ D ⓑ R
Q3. ⓐ	Q10. ⓒ	Q17. ⓐ R ⓑ D
Q4. ⓑ	Q11. ⓑ	Q18. ⓐ R ⓑ D
Q5. ⓐ	Q12. ⓒ	Q19. ⓐ D ⓑ R
Q6. ⓒ	Q13. ⓐ	Q20. ⓐ R ⓑ D
Q7. ⓐ	Q14. ⓐ	

Real Experiences by Korean Learners

This anecdote shared by Cassie, USA

Once, at a grocery store in Korea, I was looking for honey in the syrup aisle, but I couldn't find it. So I asked a clerk who was stocking shelves, and he looked at me funny until my Korean friend who was with me asked again. Turns out I had said, "굴 어디에 있어요?" which means, "Where are the oysters?" 꿀 is the word for honey.

The importance of proper pronunciation!

How To Sound Like A Native Korean Speaker

CHAPTER 9.

That Is Not My Name.

These are the names of the TTMIK team members. Which name is the most difficult for you to pronounce?

주연 　 경화 　 현우 　 윤아

화연 　 보람 　 은희 　 경은 　 준배

예지 　 캐시 　 석진 　 다혜

A while back, we asked this same question on our social media, and our followers chose 은희 as the hardest name to pronounce. It may have seemed more difficult because of the unfamiliar vowels ㅡ and ㅢ, but if you have been studying with this book from Chapter 1 then it probably is not so difficult for you.

● **Shall we try pronouncing 은희?**

은희

 Listen to the native speaker's pronunciation.
01

What do you think? Was your pronunciation similar to the native speaker's? In this lesson we will practice how to properly pronounce Korean names. This is also an opportunity for you to use the rules you have been learning starting from Chapter 1 until now. Two birds, one stone, right?

First, let's practice with an easy name. On our social media last time, people voted for 보람 as the easiest name to pronounce. 보람 is a word that means "the good feelings or results gained after doing something", but it is also a common Korean name.

● Shall we try pronouncing it?

보람

▶ Listen to the native speaker's pronunciation.
02

● Paying attention to the pronunciation of ㅂ and ㄹ, listen to the native speaker's pronunciation once more and follow along.

Next, let's try pronouncing Seokjin's name.

석진

If you look at Seokjin's name, after the final consonant ㄱ there is a ㅈ. How should we pronounce this ㅈ? That is right. In Chapter 4 Lesson 1, we learned that when ㅈ comes after the final consonant ㄱ, the ㅈ is pronounced as [ㅉ].

▶ Listen to the native speaker's pronunciation and follow along.
03

석진 [석찐] 선생님!

● Next, let's practice 윤아 and 현우.

윤아　　현우

For both of these names, after the final consonant ㄴ there is a vowel. Because the final consonant that comes before a vowel is pronounced together with the vowel in the following syllable, these two names should be pronounced [유나] and [허누].

▶ **Listen to the native speaker's pronunciation and follow along.**
04

윤아 [유나]　　현우 [허누]

Also, in Chapter 1 Lesson 2, we practiced comparing the pronunciations of ㅠ and ㅕ, right? Hyunwoo's name has the vowel ㅕ.

● **Let's practice pronouncing Hyunwoo's name again, paying attention to the ㅕ.**

현우 [허누] 선생님

There is also a ㅕ in Kyunghwa's name.

▶ **Try reading Kyunghwa's name.**
05

경화

● **Great. Now let's practice Kyeong-eun's name.**

경은

▶ Because many people have difficulties with the pronunciation of 으, try practicing pronouncing 으 first, then 은. Then we will try pronouncing 경은.

으

▶ Now, let's pronounce it with the final consonant 은.

은

경은

Since we have practiced 은, the 은희 should be no problem. What is that? Is it still difficult because of the ㅢ in 희?

In Chapter 3, we learned that when there is "a consonant + ㅢ", the ㅢ is pronounced as ㅣ. So, you can simply pronounce 희 as [히]. When you thought it had to be pronounced [희] it probably seemed difficult, but the pronunciation of 은희 is not actually as difficult as you thought, right?

▶ Let's practice.

은희 [은히]

However, some native speakers pronounce the ㅎ that comes after a nasal consonant sound (ㄴ, ㅁ, or ㅇ), such as the ㅎ in 은희, very softly, if at all, and pronounce the final consonant with the vowel of the following syllable. This pronunciation sounds like [으니]. This is because it is easier to pronounce that way.

This is similar to how Korean words like 은행 and 전화번호 are often pronounced. There are cases where even if the ㅎ is pronounced, it is so weak that you can barely hear it. It is good to know this for reference!

Lastly, let's pronounce the name 다혜, which was considered just as difficult as 은희. Many people actually asked us how to read 다혜. We think this might be because the character 혜 looks a bit complicated.

다혜

First, let's practice by saying Yeji's name, which has the same vowel, ㅖ, but has no consonant. 예 can be pronounced by pronouncing 이 and quickly switching to 에.

▶ **Let's practice them below, in order.**
09

예 ➡ 예지　　　혜 ➡ 다혜

▶ **If you happen to be having trouble pronouncing [혜], you can pronounce**
10 **it as [헤]. Actually, with the exception of 예 and 례, native speakers often pronounce ㅖ as [ㅔ] because it is easier to say.**

다혜 [다헤] 선생님

Great. Now let's practice with some other names. In Korea, when you call someone by name, you do not just say their name, but you also add something like 씨, 님, –아/야, or 선생님 at the end.

▶ **This time, let's practice adding these endings to people's names.**
11

주연 선생님 [주연 선생님]

준배 님 [준배 님]

석준아 [석쭈나]

희주야 [히주야]

은혜 씨 [은혜 씨] / [은헤 씨]

승완 선생님 [승완 선생님]

We will practice including last names as well. In Korea, many people have one of the following four last names: 김, 이, 박, or 최. 김 is much like the American surname "Smith" in that it is a very common last name in Korea.

Let's try practicing these four surname, as well as the surnames of the TTMIK team members: 강, 유, 선, 석, 진, 문, and 한.

김 이 박 최
강 유 선 석 진 문 한

Now, let's practice with both first and last names. How should we pronounce the names of the three people below?

Pay attention to the first sound of the second syllable and try reading out the three names.

석다혜   박주연   박희주

In the first two names, the ㄷ and ㅈ after ㄱ should be pronounced as [ㄸ] and [ㅉ] (Chapter 4, Lesson 1). In the third name, "ㄱ + ㅎ" should be pronounced as [ㅋ] (Chapter 4, Lesson 6).

▶ Now, after checking the native speaker's pronunciation, try reading the three
13
names again.

석다혜 [석따혜] / [석따헤]

박주연 [박쭈연]

박희주 [바키주]

However, when letting someone know a person's exact name syllable by syllable, the names would be pronounced as [석다혜], [박주연], and [박히주].

▶ **Below is a list of first and last names. Which names do you think go together?**

14, 15 **Connect them. After that, read the first and last names you have connected.**

(You can listen to the pronunciation of the surnames in [Track 14] and the pronunciation of the first names in [Track 15].)

이 •	• 두루
김 •	• 현우
박 •	• 석진
최 •	• 주연
유 •	• 경화
선 •	• 경은
석 •	• 승완
진 •	• 희주
문 •	• 은희
한 •	• 예지
강 •	• 다혜

Real Experiences by Korean Learners

This anecdote shared by Long, Germany

I wanted to ask a friend to write down a word that she said,

so I asked, "죽어 줄래?" instead of, "적어 줄래?"

CHAPTER 10

Do Not Get Lost On Your Way to Costco.

● Read the brand name below.

Hyundai

You have probably seen this written in English a lot. Did you know that this brand is a Korean company? How did you just pronounce this brand name?

① [하이언다이]
② [현다이]
③ [훈다이]
④ [히윤다이]
⑤ [현대]

Hyundai is the English name for 현대.

▶ **Listen to the native speaker's pronunciation.**
01

If we were to write 현대 following English romanization rules, it would be spelled "hyeondae". However, this business romanized their name as "Hyundai", so it seems that there are many people who do not pronounce is as [현:대] and pronounce it incorrectly instead. If you look at "*ai*" in the romanized word especially, it is not easy to tell that you should pronounce it as ㅐ.

This becomes a problem when you mention Hyundai to a Korean person and you pronounce it as ①, ②, ③, or ④, because Koreans are not be able to understand this pronunciation at all.

So **in this chapter, we will practice pronouncing some brand names**. We will practice not just Korean brand names like 현대, but also some other international brands as well. As we learned in Chapter 8, it is helpful to know how to pronounce the English alphabet in a Korean way.

Take a look at the title of this chapter. What would happen if you got lost on your way to Costco in Korea, and needed to ask a passerby for directions? Or what if you were riding the bus to Costco and needed to ask the driver which stop to get off at?

In these types of situations, if you were to pronounce Costco the way it is pronounced in English, you might not be understandable in Korean. So how should it be pronounced, you might ask? In Korea, we call Costco, "코스트코". When pronouncing Costco in English, the *t* sound is not really audible, but when it is pronounced in a Korean way, you can hear the 트 sound clearly.

▶ **Listen and follow along.**

02

코스트코

You do not need to enunciate every syllable individually like 코, 스, 트, 코. The 스 in particular is pronounced very quickly.

Let's practice with some other international brands that have branches in Korea.

▶ **Listen to the native speaker's pronunciation and follow along.**

03

IKEA
이케아 [이케아]

* Similar to the Swedish pronunciation, the first letter "i" is pronounced as 이.

Burger King
버거킹 [버거킹]
* The *r* sound has disappeared, right?

McDonald's
맥도날드 [맥또날드]
* The ㄷ that is linked after the final consonant ㄱ is pronounced as [ㄸ].

Starbucks
스타벅스 [스타벅쓰]
* The ㅅ that is linked after the final consonant ㄱ is pronounced as [ㅆ].

Subway
써브웨이 [써브웨이]
* The first sound is not ㅅ, but rather ㅆ.

Shake Shack
쉐이크쉑 [쉑쉑]
* It is written as 쉐이크쉑, but when saying it aloud, people pronounce it as 쉑쉑.

Estée Lauder
에스티 로더 [에스티 로더]

How To Sound Like A Native Korean Speaker

Lacoste
라코스테 [라코스테]
* Sometimes it is also pronounced as [라꼬스떼].

This time, let's practice pronouncing some Korean brand names. First is a well-known car company like the one we looked at earlier, Hyundai. Let's practice the Korean pronunciation of Kia.

▶ **Listen to the native speaker's pronunciation and follow along.**
04

Kia [기아]

Hyundai [현:대]

Next, let's look at some companies famous for electronics.

Samsung [삼성]

LG [엘지]

In English, "Sam" is pronounced similarly to 쌤, so there are many people who pronounce Samsung as [쌤썽]. But the correct pronunciation is actually [삼성]. The 삼 in 삼성 means "three", as in "일, 이, 삼...". This is the same 삼!

▶ **Let's listen to the native speaker's pronunciation and follow along.**
05

This time, let's look at the name of a bank.

Among the various banks in Korea, we selected two that many people have difficulty pronouncing correctly. As expected, it is an issue that arises from reading the name written in the English alphabet as if it were an English word.

Shinhan Bank
Woori Bank

The Korean names of the two banks are 신한은행 and 우리은행, but they are often mistakenly pronounced as [신핸] and [워리].

▶ **Listen to the correct pronunciation of the native speaker and follow along.**
06

신한은행
우리은행

Next, let's look at some cosmetics brands. Have you started to grasp the feeling of how to read them in Korean?

Etude House
Aritaum
Missha

Olive Young

These brands are often written using the English alphabet, not Hangeul, so before hearing how they are pronounced in Korean, you may not know how to pronounce them. The way these four brands are written in Korean is as follows:

에뛰드 하우스

아리따움

미샤

올리브영

The "t" in Etude House and Aritaum is not ㅌ, but ㄸ, right? Since we practiced this in Chapter 1, you should be able to differentiate and pronounce both ㅌ and ㄸ well.

▶ **Now, try pronouncing the brand names first, then listen to the native**
07 **speaker's pronunciation and read them again.**

Shall we move on to brands related to food? Do you like bread? There are two large bakery franchises in Korea. Their names are Paris Baguette and Tous les Jours. As expected, like the cosmetics brands we practiced above, the signs for these shops are usually written in the English alphabet rather than Korean. So it seems like if you could pronounce their names using an English or French pronunciation. However, in actuality, if you were to pronounce it that way, Koreans would not understand you at all. So let's practice the Korean pronunciation of these two bakeries.

Tous les Jours 뚜레쥬르
Paris Baguette 파리바게뜨

But wait! If we look more closely, Koreans do not pronounce 뚜레쥬르 and 파리바게뜨 exactly as they are written. In real life they are pronounced a little bit differently.

▶ **Take a listen.**

08

That is right.

뚜레쥬르 [뚜레주르]
파리바게뜨 [빠리바게트]

Koreans usually pronounce both names like this. In the case of 파리바게뜨, the full name is sometimes shortened to just 빠바.

● **Try pronouncing both out loud again, remembering what you have learned in previous chapters.**

Let's practice with sentences!

To help you get fully used to the Korean way of pronouncing these brand names even while looking at them written in English letters, we have purposely written the brand names in English.

▶ **First, read them by yourself slowly, then listen to the native speaker's pronunciation and follow along.**

09 한국 가면, Etude House에 가서 화장품 좀 사다 줘.
= If you go to Korea, go to Etude House and buy me some cosmetics.

10 LG 폰 쓰다가 Samsung으로 갈아탔어요.
= I was using an LG phone, then I switched to Samsung.

11 Shake Shack 가서 햄버거 먹을까, Subway 가서 샌드위치 먹을까?
= Shall we go to Shake Shack and have a burger, or shall we go to Subway and have a sandwich?

12 '현다이' 아니고 Hyundai예요.
= It's not 현다이, it's Hyundai.

13 우리 Tous les Jours 옆에 있는 Woori 은행 앞에서 만나자.
= Let's meet at the Woori Bank next to the Tous les Jours.

I was talking to my friend, and I said that he was 나쁜, but he thought I called him 남편. We laughed, but I was so embarrassed!

CHAPTER 11.

Correct Order,
Wrong Food

Lesson 1
Sundae Blues

● Read the following word aloud.

순대 sundae

▶ This time, let's listen to the native speaker's pronunciation.

01

So, how did you compare?

If you sounded different than the native speaker, what could be the reason why?

Could it be because of the English word next to the Hangeul? The romanized word next to the Korean can be a hindrance to pronunciation. Just looking at it, you might think that 순대 means ice cream!

In this chapter, we will use the tips you have learned in this book so far to practice pronouncing Korean food names like native speakers.

▶ Let's practice with some names that include sounds that you may have found

02 difficult.

김치찌개 [김치찌개]
떡볶이 [떡뽀끼]

빵 [빵]
보쌈 [보쌈]
깍두기 [깍뚜기]

How do we pronounce the word 닭, which means chicken?

That is right. Between the ㄹ and the ㄱ, you only need to pronounce the ㄱ, so it is pronounced [닥].

▶ **Now, shall we practice some food names that include 닭?**
03

찜닭 [찜닥]
닭갈비 [닥깔비]

Why does 닭갈비 become [닥깔비] when pronounced? Just like we learned in Chapter 6, when ㄱ, ㄷ, and ㅂ are final consonants and are followed by ㄱ, ㄷ, ㅂ, ㅅ, or ㅈ, they become [ㄲ], [ㄸ], [ㅃ], [ㅆ], [ㅉ] when pronounced.

▶ **What are some other foods with this kind of pronunciation?**
04

족발 [족빨]
비빔밥 [비빔빱]
삼겹살 [삼겹쌀]

Be especially careful when pronouncing the ㅈ in 족발 not to pronounce it like an English *j*. You remember learning the difference between the Korean consonant ㅈ and the English consonant *j* in Chapter 7, right?

▶ **Now, let's practice some more food names that contain the consonant ㅈ.**
05

전 [전]

돼지갈비 [돼:지갈비]

Be careful not to pronounce 갈비 as [갤비]. If you read the romanization exactly as it is written in English, you might have pronounced it like [갤비].

● **This time, read 갈비 in Korean out loud.**

(갈비 means "rib", but 닭갈비 does not actually refer to chicken ribs. Rather, it is called that because 닭갈비 it is a chicken dish that is prepared using the same methods used to make pork ribs.)

갈비

Also, take care not to pronounce ㄷ like the English *t* or *d*.

▶ **Listen to the native speaker's pronunciation of the following words.**
06

두부

된장

▶ **What are some dishes that have tofu or bean paste in them?**
07

된장찌개 [된:장찌개]

순두부찌개 [순두부찌개]

Now that you have had plenty of practice, shall we try ordering at a restaurant?

(▶) **Listen and repeat.**

08 **김치찌개 하나 주세요.**

= One kimchi stew, please.

09 **삼겹살 3인분 주세요.**

= Three orders of pork belly, please.

10 **여기 깍두기 좀 더 주세요.**

= Could you please bring us some more radish kimchi?

11 **찜닭 큰 거 주세요.**

= A large order of braised chicken, please.

12 **돼지갈비 2인분 주세요.**

= Two orders of pork ribs, please.

Lesson 2

Why Are Olives So Hard to Find?

In Lesson 1, we learned how to pronounce the Korean food "순대 [sundae]", which is not an ice cream sundae. Then what is "ice cream" in Korean, and how do we pronounce it?

"Ice cream" in Korean is the same as the English word: 아이스크림.

So, then, how does the pronunciation of 아이스크림 in Korean differ from the English pronunciation of "ice cream"?

▶ **Listen to the native speaker.**
01

ice cream 아이스크림

What do you think? How is it different?
Right. "Ice cream" has two syllables, but 아이스크림 has five syllables.

▶ **Paying attention to the pronunciation of both the vowel ― and the consonant**
02 **ㄹ, try following along.**

아이스크림

In this lesson, you will use the loanword pronunciation tips you learned in Chapter 8 to pronounce food name loanwords like Koreans do!

▶ 03 First, let's practice with the names of some foods that contains the vowel ㅡ, like in 아이스크림.

cheese 치즈 [치즈]

juice 주스 [주쓰]

salad 샐러드 [쌜러드]

soup 수프 [수프]

steak 스테이크 [스테이크]

yogurt 요거트 [요거트]

▶ 04 Now, let's practice with the names of foods containing the vowel l instead of ㅡ.

sausage 소시지 [쏘시지]

orange 오렌지 [오렌지]

sandwich 샌드위치 [쌘드위치]

As we learned in Chapter 7, when pronouncing 아이스크림 or 오렌지, the pronunciation of the Hangeul ㄹ in Korean is a little different than the way *r* is pronounced in "ice cream" or "orange" in English.

▶ **Shall we practice some more examples in which *r* changes to ㄹ?**
05

Americano 아메리카노 [아메리카노]

churros 추로스 [추로스/추러스]

risotto 리소토 [리조토/리조또]

▶ **Now, let's take a look at some words where the English *v* is changed to the**
06 **Hangeul ㅂ.**

vitamin 비타민 [비타민]

vanilla 바닐라 [바닐라]

olive 올리브 [올리브]

In the case of words like 올리브, is it important to clearly pronounce the ㅂ as well as the ㅡ vowel. If you do not clearly pronounce both, people at the grocery store will not know what you are talking about when you ask where the olives are.

▶ **Finally, let's practice some words where the *f* sound changes to ㅍ.**
07

coffee 커피 [커피]

caffe latte 카페 라테 [카페 라떼/까페 라떼]

waffle 와플 [와플]

Great job! Are you feeling more comfortable pronouncing English words using Korean pronunciation now? Have you ever been in a situation where you thought you pronounced an English word with the correct Korean pronunciation, but the listener could not understand you? When that happens, it may not have been the pronunciation itself, but rather the intonation of the word.

▶ This time, let's practice not just pronunciation but also intonation by imitating the audio.

08

치즈 [치즈]   주스 [주쓰]   샐러드 [쌜러드]

수프 [수프]   스테이크 [스테이크] 요거트 [요거트]

소시지 [쏘시지]   오렌지 [오렌지]   샌드위치 [쌘드위치]

아메리카노 [아메리카노]   추로스 [추로스/추러스]

리소토 [리조토/리조또]   비타민 [비타민]

바닐라 [바닐라]   올리브 [올리브]   커피 [커피]

카페 라테 [카페 라떼/까페 라떼]   와플 [와플]

Now, shall we practice with some sentences that can be used in real life?

▶ Listen and repeat.

09 치즈는 어디에 있어요?

= Where is the cheese?

10 여기 스테이크 맛있어요?

= Is the steak good here?

11 샌드위치 하나 포장해 주세요.

= One sandwich to go, please.

12 비타민 좀 먹어요.

= Take some vitamins.

13 아메리카노 한 잔 주세요.

= One Americano, please.

14 와플 먹을래요?

= Do you want a waffle?

CHAPTER 12.

There Is No Gang in Gangnam.

Gangnam

This neighborhood has become very famous thanks to a certain singer's song. But how do you pronounce Gangnam? [갱냄]? [갱남]? [강남]? We will give you a hint: the answer is contained in the title of this lesson, "There's No Gang in Gangnam." How do Koreans pronounce Gangnam without "gang"?

▶ **Take a listen.**

01

Gangnam in Korean is written as 강남 and read as [강남]. If you were to look at 강남 written in Korean, you probably would not pronounce it as [갱남], but when looking at it written in English letters, it is easier to read it with an English pronunciation, right? In this lesson we will practice pronouncing some Korean place names. You will both learn the Hangeul writing of place names that you might have only seen written in English until now, and also learn to pronounce them properly in Korean.

First, shall we practice with the capital of South Korea, Seoul?

Seoul
서울

The romanization of 서울 is [seo-ul] so the English spelling, Seoul, seems right on point. However, Seoul is often pronounced like the English word "soul [soʊl]". This pronunciation is actually quite different from the Korean pronunciation of the name 서울.

How To Sound Like A Native Korean Speaker

Pay attention to the fact that 서울 starts with ㅅ, not ㅆ, and that while the English pronunciation of [oʊ] is one syllable, in Korean, [어우] is two syllables.Listen to the native speaker's pronunciation and follow along.

If you flew into South Korea, this is where you would land.

Incheon
인천

The "eo" that was also found in "Seoul" is in fact the romanization of the Korean vowel ㅓ .

Listen to the native speaker's pronunciation and follow along.

This time we have Busan, the second largest city in South Korea! Let's also look at Jeju Island, the largest island in South Korea and a famous sightseeing destination for many.

Let's practice the pronunciation of both in Korean.

Busan   Jeju-do
부산   제주도

Just like Gangnam is not [갱냄] but [강남], Busan is not [부샌] but [부산]. If you studied Chapter 7 Lesson 6, you will know the difference in pronunciation between "Jeju" and "제주" right away.

Let's practice again. This time, we have a place that many people living in Seoul enjoy traveling to because it is close to Seoul and is known for its beautiful mountains and beaches.

- Let's practice saying Gangwon-do. We learned "gang" in Gangnam and "do" in Jeju-do, so try to fill in the blanks with the correct vowels.

Gangwon-do

Of the many cities in Gangwon-do, one of the most famous is a city known for a chicken dish called 닭갈비. We learned about this dish in Chapter 11 Lesson 1 as well. This city is named Chuncheon, and many people learning Korean end up mispronouncing it.

- Since you now know which Korean vowel becomes "u" in the English alphabet and which vowel becomes "eo", shall we try filling in the blanks first?

Chuncheon

▶ Check the pronunciation of Gangwon-do and Chuncheon.
05

Gangwon-do Chuncheon
강원도 춘천

This time, let's practice pronouncing the names of places within Seoul that many people visit. Some of the romanizations have appeared before, and some you may be seeing for the first time.

- Try to guess which Korean spelling is the correct spelling for each place.

1. Myeongdong

ⓐ 명동　　　　　　ⓑ 명당　　　　　　ⓒ 묭동

2. Dongdaemun

ⓐ 똥대문　　　　　ⓑ 동때문　　　　　ⓒ 동대문

3. Gwanghwamun

ⓐ 광화문　　　　　ⓑ 관콰문　　　　　ⓒ 광화먼

4. Yeouido

ⓐ 유의도　　　　　ⓑ 여의도　　　　　ⓒ 유위도

5. Hapjeong

ⓐ 햅정　　　　　　ⓑ 합정　　　　　　ⓒ 햅쩡

6. Euljiro

ⓐ 이율지로　　　　ⓑ 얼지로　　　　　ⓒ 을지로

▶ Check your answers by listening and following along with the pronunciations.
06

Answers

1. ⓐ (명동)   2. ⓒ (동대문)   3. ⓐ (광화문)   4. ⓑ (여의도)   5. ⓑ (합정)   6. ⓒ (을지로)

* In the case of 합정 or 을지로, the pronunciations [합찡] and [을찌로] are correct, but the correct spelling is 합정 and 을지로.

Quiz Time!

(▶) Okay, shall we now practice with some place names that were not mentioned
Q1 above? First look at the English spelling and try filling in the Korean spelling. Once you have checked your answers, listen to the native speaker's pronunciation, and read along.

1. Suwon

2. Hongdae

How To Sound Like A Native Korean Speaker

3. Pyeongchang

4. Noryangjin

5. Ulsan

6. Sinchon

Answers

1. 수원

2. 홍대

* 홍대 is an abbreviation of the university name 홍익대학교, and refers to both the school and the neighborhood surrounding the school.

3. 평창

* Try pronouncing it while paying attention to not only the ㅕ sound, but ㅍ and ㅊ as well.

4. 노량진

* We practiced the pronunciation of ㄴ, ㄹ, and ㅈ in Chapter 7, right?

5. 울산 [울싼]

* It's written as 울산 but it is pronounced as [울싼]. Pay attention to the pronunciation of ㅆ as you try pronouncing it.

6. 신촌

* There is also a place in Seoul called 신천, so you must be careful to differentiate between the pronunciation of ㅗ and ㅓ. 신촌 and 신천 are on opposite ends of Seoul so if you were to get in a taxi and say the wrong one, you would be in trouble!

Let's practice with sentences!

▶ First read the romanized place names. Even though they are written in the English alphabet, don't forget to pronounce according to Korean pronunciation rules. Then, listen to the native speaker's pronunciation and follow along.

Q2. 기사님, **Sinchon** 가 주세요.

= Driver, take me to Sinchon please.

Q3. **Hapjeong**이랑 **Hongdae** 근처에 놀 데가 많아요.

= There are lots of places to hang out around Hapjeong and Hongdae.

Q4. **Myeongdong**에 쇼핑하러 가자.

= Let's go shopping in Myeongdong.

Q5. **Gangnam**에서 **Suwon** 화성 가는 버스 있어요?

= Is there a bus that goes to Hwaseong (Fortress) in Suwon from Gangnam?

Q6. 제 친구는 집은 **Chuncheon**에 있고, 회사는 **Seoul**에 있어요.

= My friend's house is in Chuncheon, and their office is in Seoul.

Real Experiences by Korean Learners

This anecdote shared by 데미, USA

I was hanging out with my Korean friend, and I said, "추워요!" She looked at me and said, "좋아요? What is good?" I said, "Wait! I said it's cold." She replied, "Oh you mean 추워요, not 좋아요." I was so embarrassed. I didn't understand why it sounded like 좋아요 when I said it.

CHAPTER 13.

To Avoid Stress, Correct Your Stress

Lesson 1

Highs and Lows

So far in this book, we have focused on practicing saying Korean consonants and vowels that are often difficult to pronounce for Korean learners. After much practice, you must have improved so much! However, some of you might still feel that your pronunciation does not sound like that of a native speaker, even though you are following the pronunciation rules exactly. The reason for this might be because of your intonation or speaking speed.

Of course, intonation in Korean can vary from region to region and from person to person, but if your intonation is too awkward, the listener may focus more on your accent than on what you are saying. For that reason, practicing imitating the most common intonations used by the majority of Korean speakers helps to communicate more smoothly.

In the case of speed, speaking quickly also plays a part in making you sound more fluent, but more important is your tempo when speaking. In other words, what parts are spoken in one breath, what parts are spoken quickly, what parts are spoken slowly, where you pause, etc.

한국어를 더 열심히 공부했어요.

= I studied Korean even harder.

● **Try reading the sentence aloud again, and mark the places where you pause or rest with /.**

한국어를 더 열심히 공부했어요.

What places did you mark?

(▶) **This time, listen to the native speaker.**

01

What do you think? Where did the native speaker rest? Does it seem like there are no rests? "Rests" here do not refer to long pauses, but rather to very short breaks.

Are you thinking that maybe you can just rest during the spaces between words?

한국어를 / 더 / 열심히 / 공부했어요.

Of course, when you are deliberately speaking slowly, you can speak in this way. However, **even if there are spaces between written words, there are certain words that are always linked together and said as if they were one expression when speaking.**

Below is the way that the majority of Koreans rest when saying this sentence.

한국어를 / 더 열심히 / 공부했어요.

더 modifies the meaning of 열심히, so resting between 더 and 열심히 sounds awkward.

For example, if you were to read the sentence like this, it would sound strange.

한국어를 더 / 열심히 공부했어요. (unnatural)

Also, many Korean learners rest between the noun and –하다 when saying "noun + –하다" verbs such as 공부하다. This also sounds very awkward.

한국어를 더 / 열심히 공부/했어요. (unnatural)

Of course, there are some situations where it does sound natural to rest between the noun and –하다. For example, if you are hesitating to say that you studied, you might pause between the noun and –하다, and say, "공부... 했어요." Or if someone asks if you have not studied and you want to reply that you did indeed study, you might say, "공부 (진짜) 했어요!" However, overall it generally sounds strange to rest between the noun and –하다. We will go over the reason why in more detail in just a moment.

Shall we practice with some other sentences?
Read the sentences below aloud and mark the places where you rest with /.

다혜 씨는 부모님과 한집에 살아요.
= Dahye lives with her parents.

저는 대학에서 프랑스어를 가르치고 있어요.
= I am teaching French in college.

예지 씨는 주말마다 친구들을 만나요.
= Yeji sees her friends every weekend.

▶ **Now, listen to the native speaker's pronunciation, and as you follow along,
02 compare your resting spots with theirs.**

* The vast majority of Korean native speakers say these sentences with rests like seen below.

다혜 씨는 / 부모님과 / 한집에 살아요.

저는 / 대학에서 / 프랑스어를 가르치고 있어요.

예지 씨는 / 주말마다 / 친구들을 만나요.

Now, shall we look at the rise and fall of pitches?

Let's take the sentence, "한국어를 더 열심히 공부했어요", and break it into
three segments: 한국어를, 더 열심히, and 공부했어요. Each segment can be
seen as four syllables. In Korean, these four syllable patterns usually appear
as HHLH or LHLH. Here, H is a high pitch and L is a low pitch.

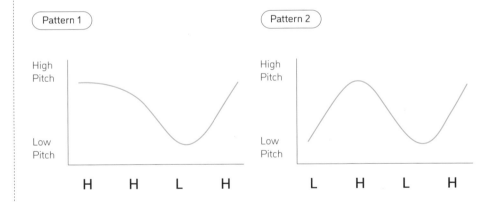

Whether the first syllable among the four starts with a high pitch or a low pitch is related to the first consonant of the syllable.

If the first consonant of the first syllable is one of the following, usually we see the HHLH pattern.

ㄲ, ㄸ, ㅃ, ㅆ, ㅉ
_____

ㅋ, ㅌ, ㅍ, ㅊ
_____

ㅅ, ㅎ
_____

⋮

H H L H

In the remaining cases, we see the LHLH pattern.

ㄱ, ㄷ, ㅂ, ㅈ
_____

ㄴ, ㅁ, ㄹ
_____

All vowels
_____

⋮

L H L H

Even if one segment is not four syllables, whether it begins with a high or low pitch is decided by the first sound of the first syllable. Of course, these pitch patterns are not absolute, but if you practice and remember the rules above you will be able to speak with a more natural intonation.

● Now, let's practice. Shall we try saying 한국어를, which we practiced earlier?

한국어를

The first syllable, 한, starts with ㅎ so we need to say it with the HHLH pattern.

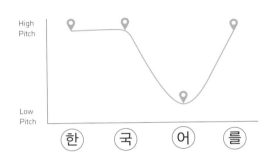

▶ To check if your intonation was natural, listen to the native speaker's pronunciation.

03

한국어 is actually one of the expressions that Korean learners frequently say with the wrong intonation. 한 should start with a high pitch, but many people say it with a low pitch.

▶ Like this, for example.

04

▶ This time, listen to 한국어 said by three different native speakers and follow along.

05

Great job. Shall we practice some more?

▶ Let's practice some expressions from the sentences we covered earlier. Listen and follow along.

06

살아요
프랑스어를

친구들을
부모님과
대학에서
주말마다

Great job.

What do you think? 살아요, 프랑스어를, and 친구들을 were all said with a high pitch on the first syllable, right? This is because the first sound of the first syllables are ㅅ, ㅍ, and ㅊ. Conversely, 부모님과, 대학에서, and 주말마다 all started with a low pitch on the first syllable.

If you were to ask why the resting points we covered at the beginning of this lesson are important, it is because of these intonation patterns. Shall we go back to 공부했어요? Imagine if you were to say 공부했어요 in one breath, and then if you were to say it in two breaths as 공부, 했어요.

공부했어요.
공부/했어요.

Because the first sound of the first syllable of 공부했어요 is ㄱ, the full 공부했어요 would be said with the intonation pattern LHLH. However, if you say 공부, rest, and then say 했어요, the intonation pattern begins again with 했어요. Because of the ㅎ, in this instance 했어요 is said with the HHLH pattern.

So at 했 the tone rises sharply and therefore it sounds like you are strongly emphasizing the fact that you "did" study. Like, "I DID study!"

▶ 07 Now, **listen to the natural pronunciation of 공부했어요 by three different people and follow along.**

▶ 08 Now, **let's practice with some other –하다 verbs.**

얼마나 대단하신지를 설명했다고 얘기했어요.

= They told me that they explained how awesome he/she is.

Great job.

Lastly, Korean learners often make mistakes related to the intonation of interrogative sentences. In particular, when the interrogative can be answered with "yes" or "no", there are many instances in which the intonation is awkward.

● **Read the sentence below out loud.**

밥 먹었어요?

▶ 09 **This time listen to the native speaker's intonation.**
What parts sound different from yours?

We learned earlier that usually the intonation pattern shows up as LHLH or HHLH, right? In this sentence, the first sound of 먹 is ㅁ, so 먹었어요 needs to take on the LHLH intonation pattern. However, many Korean learners end up pronouncing the second

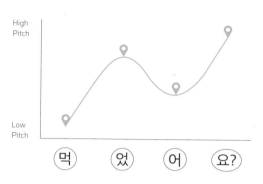

and subsequent syllables with a high tone. So rather than LHLH, they are saying it as LHHH. However, as shown in the picture below, it is natural to say 어 in a lower tone than 요. Interrogative sentences that can be answered with "yes" or "no" are usually this way.

Shall we practice with some other sentences?

10

우유 다 마셨어요?

= Have you finished the milk?

알고 있었어요?

= Did you know that?

노래방 갔어요?

= Did you go to noraebang?

Great job. Let's briefly review the three points we covered in this lesson.

(1) For segments that are said in one breath, the segment begins with a high tone when the first sound of the first syllable is one of the following: ㄲ ㄸ ㅃ ㅆ ㅉ/ㅋ ㅌ ㅍ ㅊ/ㅅ ㅎ. (Cases outside of this start with a low tone.)

(2) For verbs or adjectives with the affix −하다, do not pause before the 하 or say the 하 with a high tone (outside of times when you are purposely showing emphasis).

(3) In the case of yes or no interrogative sentences, only the last syllable of the last phrase is said with a high tone.

● **Paying attention to these three points, read the sentences below.**

▶ 희주 씨는 매운 음식을 싫어해요.
11
↳ [히주 씨는 매운 음:시글 시러해요.]

= Heeju hates spicy food.

▶ 석진 씨는 노래하고, 현우 씨는 춤을 췄어요.
12
↳ [석찐 씨는 노래하고, 혀누 씨는 추믈 춰써요.]

= Seokjin sang and Hyunwoo danced.

▶ 경화 씨가 가장 좋아하는 책이에요.
13
↳ [경화 씨가 가장 조:아하는 채기에요.]

= This is Kyunghwa's favorite book.

▶ 어제 학교에 갔어요?
14
↳ [어제 학꾜에 가써요?]

= Did you go to school yesterday?

▶ 준배 씨 미국 간 거 알고 있었어요?
15
↳ [준배 씨 미국 간 거 알:고 이써써요?]

= Did you know that Joonbae went to America?

● **Now listen to the native speaker's pronunciation and follow along.**

Lesson 2

What Did You Eat?
vs. Did You Eat Something?

뭐 먹었어요?

● Select the correct answer to the question above.

① 떡볶이 먹었어요.
② 아니요. 배고파요.

Which number is the correct answer? Number 1? Or number 2?
Actually, both of them are correct.

"뭐 먹었어요?" can actually mean both, "What did you eat?" and, "Did you eat
something?" So then how do you differentiate between the two, you might
ask? When the question is merely written down like this, it is impossible to
tell which question it is, but if you hear it spoken, it is possible to tell. This
is because there is an obvious difference in intonation depending on which
question is being asked.

▶ This time, listen to the question and select the correct answer.
01

뭐 먹었어요?

① 떡볶이 먹었어요.
② 아니요. 배고파요.

What answer did you choose? Number 1? Or number 2?

The answer is number 2.

Why is the answer number 2?

What could be the difference in intonation that indicates that "뭐 먹었어요?" means, "What did you eat?"

▶ **Let's listen to the two conversations below.**

02

1. **A:** 뭐 먹었어요? = What did you eat?
    B: 떡볶이 먹었어요. = I ate tteokbokki.

2. **A:** 뭐 먹었어요? = Did you eat something?
    B: 아니요. 배고파요. = No. I'm hungry.

What do you think? Can you tell the difference in intonation?

If we look at "뭐 먹었어요?" in the first conversation, 뭐 meaning "what" is emphasized because the question is asking what someone ate.

▶ **Listen again and follow along.**

03

뭐 먹었어요? What did you eat?

Now let's look at "뭐 먹었어요?" in the second conversation. This question is not asking what someone ate, but is asking whether someone has had a meal or if they've eaten anything yet. It is similar to the question Koreans often ask each other, "밥 먹었어요?" Because of its meaning of inquiring whether

How To Sound Like A Native Korean Speaker

someone ate or not, the focus is not on 뭐 but rather is on "먹었어요?".
Therefore, 먹었어요 is emphasized. In particular, the 먹 part in "먹었어요?" is
emphasized.

However! Just because you emphasize the 먹 in 먹었어요 doesn't mean you
need to say it in a high tone. Compared to the 먹 from the first "뭐 먹었어요?"
that means, "What did you eat?", you should say the 먹 in the second question
in a much lower tone.

▶ **Take a listen.**
04

뭐 먹었어요? Did you eat something?

"먹었어요?" here sounds close
to the LHLH pattern we learned
in the previous lesson.

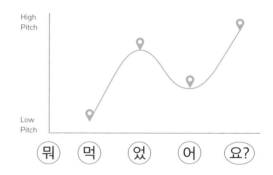

▶ **Now listen to the native speaker's pronunciation again and follow along.**
05

The meaning of the interrogative in an interrogative sentence can change
depending on intonation. Interrogative words are words such as "누구
(= who)", "언제 (= when)", "어디 (= where)", and "무엇 (= what)".

This time, let's practice with a question that uses the interrogative 언제.

▶ **First, listen to the audio and connect the matching answers.**

06

1. 언제 갈래요?	**2.** 언제 갈래요?
Response: ( )	Response: ( )

ⓐ 네, 좋아요.
ⓑ 다음 주 금요일에 가요.

Answers   1. ⓑ 2. ⓐ

Did you get them right? In number 1, the emphasis on 언제 indicates that the meaning is, "When shall we go/visit?" In number 2, the emphasis on 갈래요 indicates that the sentence means, "Shall we go/visit someday?"

● **Listen again and follow along.**

Now try reading some more sentences aloud to practice intonation.

▶ **Listen to the native speaker's intonation and follow along.**

07

"Wh" questions	Yes/No questions
누가 마셨어요? Who drank it?	누가 **마셨어요**? Did someone drink it?
누구 만나요? Who are you meeing?	누구 **만나요**? Are you meeting someone?
어디 가요? Where are you going?	어디 **가요**? Are you going somewhere?

언제 만날래요? When shall we meet?	언제 **만날래요**? Shall we meet someday?
뭘 찾으세요? What are you looking for?	뭘 **찾으세요**? Are you looking for something?
뭐 해요? What are you doing?	뭐 **해요***? Are you doing something?
언제 한국에 가요? When are you going to Korea?	언제 **한국에 가요***? Are you going to Korea someday?

* We said that the first syllable of the expression directly following the interrogative of a yes or no question should be pronounced with a low tone. However, in the case of "뭐 해요?" and "언제 한국에 가요?" because the first syllable of the expression following the interrogative starts with ㅎ, it is pronounced with a high tone like we learned in the previous lesson.

Quiz Time!

Now that you have gotten used to the differences in intonation, shall we try answering a quiz?

▶ Listen to the questions and choose the appropriate response.

Q1. 밖에 누가 있어요?

ⓐ 다혜 씨가 있어요.

ⓑ 아니요, 아무도 없어요.

Q2. 우리 뭐 먹을래요?

ⓐ 아니요, 지금은 배불러요.

ⓑ 김치찌개 어때요?

Q3. 경화 씨, 지금 뭐 해요?

ⓐ 음악 들어요.

ⓑ 아니요. 왜요?

▶ Listen to the audio for ⓐ and ⓑ, then choose which intonation of the two fits with the answer said by B in the dialogue.

Q4.

A: ＿＿＿＿＿＿＿＿＿＿＿＿   ⓐ 뭐 마실래요?   ⓑ 뭐 마실래요?

B: 아니요. 목 안 말라요.

Q5.

A: ＿＿＿＿＿＿＿＿＿＿＿＿   ⓐ 누가 안 왔어요?   ⓑ 누가 안 왔어요?

B: 은희 씨가 안 왔어요.

Q6.

A: ＿＿＿＿＿＿＿＿＿＿＿＿   ⓐ 언제 만날래요?   ⓑ 언제 만날래요?

B: 내일 어때요?

Q7.

Listen to the three conversations and circle the one where the question and answer does not match.

① **A:** 뭐 먹고 싶어요?

    B: 아니요. 현우 씨는요?

② **A:** 누구 기다려요?

    B: 화연 씨 기다려요.

③ **A:** 경화 씨 어디 갔어요?

    B: 네. 아까 나갔어요.

Let's practice through dialogues!

First, listen to the native speakers' pronunciation of the conversation. Then listen again, and say the sentences out loud at the same time as the native speakers. Keep practicing until it sounds natural!

Q8.

A: 우리 뭐 먹을래요?

    ↳ [우리 뭐: 머글래요?]

    = Shall we eat something?

B: 아니요. 지금은 배불러요. 퇴근하고 저녁 먹어요.

    ↳ [아니요. 지그믄 배불러요. 퇴:근하고 저녁 머거요.]

    = No. I'm full now. Let's have dinner after work.

A: 좋아요. 뭐 먹을래요?

    ↳ [조:아요. 뭐: 머글래요?]

    = Sounds good. What shall we eat?

B: 음... 피자 어때요?

= Umm... How about pizza?

Q9.

A: 얼굴이 많이 탔네요. 어디 갔다 왔어요?

↳ [얼구리 마:니 탄네요. 어디 갇따 와써요?]

= Your face is so tan. Did you go somewhere?

B: 네. 주말에 제주도 갔다 왔어요.

↳ [네. 주마레 제:주도 갇따 와써요.]

= Yes. I went to Jeju island over the weekend.

A: 우와, 부러워요. 제주도에서 어디 갔다 왔어요?

↳ [우와, 부러워요. 제:주도에서 어디 갇따 와써요?]

= Wow, I'm jealous. Where did you go on Jeju island?

B: 한라산이랑 바닷가요.

↳ [할:라사니랑 바닫까요.]

= I went to Hallasan and the beach.

Q10.

A: 왜 출발 안 해요? 누가 안 왔어요?

↳ [왜: 출발 안 해요? 누가 아놔써요?]

= Why aren't we leaving? Has someone not arrived?

B: 네. 아직 안 온 사람이 있대요.

↳ [네. 아직 아논 사:라미 읻때요.]

= Yes. They say someone hasn't arrived yet.

A: 누가 안 왔어요?

↳ [누가 아놔써요?]

= Who hasn't arrived?

How To Sound Like A Native Korean Speaker

c: 다혜 씨가 아직 안 왔어요.

    ↳ [다혜 씨가 아직 아나써요.]

= Dahye hasn't arrived yet.

Q11.

A: 경화 씨, 뭐 마실래요?

= Kyung-hwa, would you like something to drink?

B: 네. 목이 마르네요.

    ↳ [네. 모기 마르네요.]

= Yes. I am thirsty.

A: 뭐 마실래요? 커피? 차?

= What would you like to drink? Coffee? Tea?

B: 그냥 물 한 잔만 주세요.

= Just a glass of water, please.

Answers

Q1. ⓐ Q2. ⓐ Q3. ⓑ Q4. ⓐ Q5. ⓑ Q6. ⓐ Q7. ①

Real Experiences by Korean Learners

This anecdote shared by Júlia Morelli, Brazil

I graduated with a degree in Visual Arts, and during my last semester I got a scholarship for a summer program in Korea. At that time, I was working as a freelance illustrator. When I was asked in Korea if I had a job besides going to college, I said that I sold drawings. But my pronunciation was not very good, so I said 크림 instead of 그림, so the person thought that I was selling "cream". This was so embarrassing because this person thought I was buying creams in Korea to sell in Brazil, but I just wanted to say that I sold drawings.

How To Sound Like A Native Korean Speaker

CHAPTER 14

The Dictionary Is Wrong?!

▶ Listen to the audio and choose the word that fills in the blank.
01

이거 _____ 야. This is mine.

① 내 거
② 내 꺼

The native speaker said [내 꺼]. However, the word in the blank is number 1. Native speakers pronounce the 거 in "내 거 (= mine)", "누구 거 (= whose)", and "석진이 거 (= Seokjin's)" as [꺼] instead of [거], despite the fact that the standard pronunciation of 거 in the dictionary is [거]. The 거 used in these sentence is not the 거 that means "thing", but is the 거 that means "possession".

▶ Practice by putting each of the words in the underlined space one by one.
02

_____ 거 [꺼]

① 내
② 누구
③ 석진이

In this lesson, we will look at words that native speakers pronounce differently from the standard pronunciation. (As you may remember, we looked at loanwords that native speakers pronounce differently from their dictionary notations in Chapter 8 Lesson 3 as well.) Since this is something that cannot be understood unless we listen and practice a lot, shall we listen and repeat several times?

How To Sound Like A Native Korean Speaker

First, let's take a look at cases in which the first sound of the second word in a phrase is hardened, such as "거 [꺼]".

When native speakers say "저번 주 (= last week)", "이번 주 (= this week)", and "다음 주 (= next week)", 주 is often pronounced as [쭈]. The same applies when "달 (= month)" comes after 저번, 이번, or 다음.

● **Shall we practice?**

▶ 03

_____ 주 [쭈]

① 저번
② 이번
③ 다음

▶ 04

_____ 달 [딸]

① 저번
② 이번
③ 다음

* For reference, if two words are combined into one word such as "매주 (= every week)", "매달 (= every month)", "지난주 (= last week)", and "지난달 (= last month)", 주 and 달 are not pronounced with a hardened sound.

동안, which means "for" or "during", is often pronounced as [똥안] rather than the standard pronunciation of [동안].

▶ 05 **Listen to the native speaker's pronunciation and follow along.**

_____ 동안 [똥안] for, during

① 한 달 one month
② 두 시간 two hours
③ 한참 a long time

* For reference, if "verb + –는" comes in front of 동안, as in 내가 없는 동안, 동안 is pronounced as [동안].

Also, the first sound of counters following the numbers "열 (10)" and "여덟 (8)" are almost always pronounced as hardened sounds.

● **Practice by putting each of the answers in the underlined space one by one.**

⊙ **열** _____
06

① 개 [깨] counter for things
② 병 [뼝] counter for bottles
③ 시 [씨] o'clock
④ 장 [짱] counter for paper

⊙ **여덟** _____
07

① 권 [꿘] counter for books
② 분 [뿐] honorific counter for people
③ 사람 [싸람] counter for people
④ 번째 [뻔째] counter for ordered numbers

● **This time, read the sentence below.**

좀 작다. 다른 거 없어?

= It's a bit small. Do you have a different one?

How should we pronounce this?

⊙ **The standard pronunciation is like this.**
08

[좀 작:따. 다른 거 업써?]

However, the first sound of the three words 좀, 작다, and 다른 tend to be pronounced as a hardened sound.

좀 [좀] a little → 좀 [쫌]

작다 [작:따] to be small → 작다 [짝:따]

다른 [다른] different → 다른 [따른]

Unlike "내 거 [내 꺼]", "열 개 [열 깨]", and "여덟 권 [여덜 꿘]", which are always pronounced hardened, these sounds above are not always hardened. However, you will often see native speakers pronounce them with hardened sounds.

If the three words above were always pronounced as hardened sounds, it
09 **would probably sound like this, right?**

[쫌 짝따. 따른 거 업써?]

Let's look at some other words similar to "좀 [쫌]", "작다 [짝:따]", and "다른 [따른]". When these types of words are used in colloquial speech, the first syllable's first sound ㄱ, ㄷ, ㅅ, or ㅈ is pronounced as [ㄲ], [ㄸ], [ㅆ], or [ㅉ].

Listen to the native speaker and follow along.

감다 [감:따] → 감다 [깜:따]
10 = to wash (hair)

Ex)
머리 감았어? = Did you wash your hair?
Standard: [머리 가마써?]
Colloquial: [머리 까마써?]

▶ 과 [과] → 과 [꽈]
11
= department

Ex)

무슨 과예요? = What department is it? / What department are you in?

Standard: [무슨 과예요?]

Colloquial: [무슨 꽈예요?]

▶ 세다 [세:다] → 세다 [쎄:다]
12
= to be strong

Ex)

세게 밀어 보세요. = Push it hard.

Standard: [세:게 미:러 보세요.]

Colloquial: [쎄:게 미:러 보세요.]

▶ 세련되다 [세:련되다] → 세련되다 [쎄:련되다]
13
= to be sophisticated

Ex)

그 영화는 지금 봐도 세련됐어요. = The movie is sophisticated, even now.

Standard: [그 영화는 지금 봐도 세:련돼써요.]

Colloquial: [그 영화는 지금 봐도 쎄:련돼써요.]

▶ 졸다 [졸:다] → 졸다 [쫄:다]
14
= to boil down

Ex)

국물이 다 졸았어요. = The broth has all boiled down.

How To Sound Like A Native Korean Speaker

Standard: [궁무리 다 조라써요.]
Colloquial: [궁무리 다 쪼라써요.]

⊙ 자르다 [자르다] → 자르다 [짜르다]
15
= to cut

Ex)
어제 머리 잘랐어요. = I cut my hair yesterday.
Standard: [어제 머리 잘랐어요.]
Colloquial: [어제 머리 짤라써요.]

⊙ 잘리다 [잘리다] → 잘리다 [짤리다]
16
= to get fired

Ex)
회사에서 잘렸어요? = Did you get fired from your company?
Standard: [회:사에서 잘려써요?]
Colloquial: [회:사에서 짤려써요?]

⊙ 닦다 [닥따] → 닦다 [딱따]
17
= to wipe, to brush

Ex)
이 닦고 자야지. = You should brush your teeth, then sleep.
Standard: [이 닥꼬 자야지.]
Colloquial: [이 딱꼬 자야지.]

The last word we will look at is 네. This is not the 네 used when saying 네 or 아니요, but rather the 네 that means "you". Huh? You may be asking, "Isn't it

너?" That is right. The Korean word for "you" is 너. However, if you add –가 to 너, it becomes 네가 instead of 너가. Similarly, if you add –가 to 나, it becomes 내가, not 나가. Likewise, if you add 너 and –의 to make 너의, 너의 is shortened to 네.

$$나 + -가 = 내가$$

$$너 + -가 = 네가$$

$$나 + -의 = 나의 = 내$$

$$너 + -의 = 너의 = 네$$

However, perhaps because this 네, meaning "you", has the same pronunciation as the 내 that means "I", many people pronounce this 네 as [니] rather than [네].

네가 you are

Standard: [네가]
Colloquial: [니가]

네 your

Standard: [네]
Colloquial: [니]

● Now, listen to the native speaker's pronunciation of the sentences below and follow along.

▶ 네가 먼저 해. You go first.
18

Standard: [네가 먼저 해.]
Colloquial: [니가 먼저 해.]

▶ 네 동생 귀엽다. Your younger sibling is cute.
19

Standard: [네 동생 귀ː엽따.]
Colloquial: [니 동생 귀ː엽따.]

Let's practice with sentences!

Now, let's put the words we learned earlier into dialogues and practice. Click on the audio track to listen. First, read part B after the native speaker says part A, as if you are having a conversation with the native speaker. Then, switch roles. You will read part A first, and then the native speaker will say part B. For the phrases that have blanks below them, practice with the colloquial pronunciation rather than the standard pronunciation.

▶ 1.
20
A: 이거 누구 거야? = Whose is this?

[   ]

B: 네 거 아니야? = Isn't it yours?

[   ]

A: 내 거 아닌데? = It's not mine.

[   ]

21
2.

A: 이 옷 진짜 작다. 동생 거예요?

[   ][   ]

= These clothes are so small. Are they your younger sibling's?

B: 아니요. 제 거예요. 저번 주에 샀어요.

[   ]   [   ]

= No. They're mine. I bought them last week.

22
3.

A: 저 사람 우리 과 학생인가?

[   ]

= Is that person a student in our department?

B: 글쎄. 다른 과 학생인 것 같은데?

[   ]

= I don't know. I think they're a student from a different department.

23
4.

A: 책 몇 권 빌릴 거예요?

[   ]

= How many books are you going to borrow?

B: 여덟 권이요.

[   ]

= Eight books.

A: **다음 주까지** 다 읽을 수 있어요?

[   ]

= Can you read them all by next week?

B: 네? 이 책들 **한 달 동안** 빌리는 거예요.

[   ]

= Huh? These books can be borrowed for a month.

A: 아, 그러면 **다음** 달에 반납하면 돼요?

[   ]

= Oh, so you just return them next month?

B: 네, 맞아요. = Yes. That's right.

Colloquial Pronunciation

1. 누구 거 [누구 꺼], 네 거 [니 꺼], 내 거 [내 꺼]

2. 작다 [짝:따], 동생 거 [동생 꺼], 제 거 [제 꺼], 저번 주 [저:번 쭈]

3. 과 [꽈], 다른 과 [따른 꽈]

4. 몇 권 [멷 꿘], 여덟 권 [여덜 꿘], 다음 주 [다음 쭈], 한 달 동안 [한 달 똥안], 다음 달 [다음 딸]

Real Experiences by Korean Learners

This anecdote shared by Veronica, Canada

We were visiting Korea for a while and would often get our groceries at HomePlus. The branch we went to was giant, and it was really hard for us to find anything. On our first visit we wanted to buy some rice, so we found this older lady near the deli/meat section and decided to ask her about it. She had such a shocked expression. It took us a while to realise we were asking for 살 (human flesh) instead of 쌀.

That explained her bewilderment. ^^;

BONUS :
The Short-Long Debate

Short Vowels and Long Vowels in Korean – How Important Are They?

Take a look at these pairs of English words: sit/seat, did/deed, fill/feel, hit/heat, still/steal, and fit/feet. The main distinction between the two words in each pair is the length of the vowel sound. The Korean language has words that can be paired up like this, but what makes Korean potentially tricky is that many of these "similarly sounding" words have the same spelling.

For example, if you see the word 일 written somewhere, it can mean either "number one" or "work". Of course, it is not difficult to understand the intended meaning through context, but catching the difference in pronunciation can sometimes be tricky. As you may or may not know, the standard pronunciations of the two words are actually different even though the words are spelled the same. To say the number "one", you need to say 일 with a short vowe. To say the 일 that means "work", you pronounce 일 with a longer vowel sound.

So the distinction between short vowels and long vowels in Korean definitely exists and is not very hard to understand. Below are some examples of words that you should always pronounce with the accurate vowel length in order to avoid confusion and misunderstanding. (The vowel before the : mark should be pronounced long.)

별로 not really vs. 별:로 to a star

사는 곳 a place where you buy vs. 사:는 곳 a place where you live

주사 behavior you show when you are drunk vs. 주:사 a shot or injection

말 horse vs. 말: words or language

눈 eye vs. 눈: snow

벌 punishment vs. 벌: bee

In addition to these words in which the short/long vowel distinction is important, there are also many other words that are pronounced with a long vowel but don't have a short vowel counterpart.

계:속 continuously, repeatedly (Pronouncing 계 with a short vowel is incorrect.)

그:림 drawing (Pronouncing 그 with a short vowel is incorrect.)

Then, how do you determine which syllables are pronounced with long vowels and which are pronounced with short vowels? How can you tell without having heard the pronunciation of the word before? Unfortunately, the answer is that you cannot. There is no intuitive or logical way to know why 눈 for eyes has a short vowel and why 눈 for snow has a long vowel, so it requires prior knowledge or exposure to each specific word.

For this reason, even native Korean speakers make mistakes regarding short and long vowels, and more and more people, especially younger Koreans, often do not follow the standard vowel length rules for certain words.

So our suggestion for you as a Korean learner is to try to listen to a wide variety of different accents and pronunciation styles from many different people, and form your own perceived boundaries for acceptable Korean pronunciation. And during that process, every time you come across a word and look it up in the dictionary, always check the standard phonetic symbols written next to the word as well. Don't worry too much, though—you will still be understood by most people when you say that your 눈: (long vowel, therefore meaning "snow") is hurting, when you actually want to say that your 눈 (short vowel, meaning "eye") is hurting.

GLOSSARY

-(으)ㄹ 거예요	one will...; one is going to...
-(으)ㄹ 것 같아요	I think one will...
-(으)ㄹ 때	when
-(으)ㄹ 뻔하다	to almost + V
-(으)ㄹ 수 있다	can
-(으)ㄹ 줄 알아요	one can..., one knows how to...
-(으)ㄹ게요	I will
-(으)ㄹ수록	the more... the more...
-(으)려고 하다	to plan to + V
-고	and
-고 싶다	to want to + V
-고 있다	to be + V-ing
-과	with
-권	ticket
-기 전에	before + V-ing
-기로 하다	to plan to + V
-까지	to, until
-ㄴ 것 같다	I think
-ㄴ다고 말하다	to tell someone that + S + V
-는	topic marking particle
-는 대신에	instead (of), in return for
-는 중	in the middle of V-ing
-다가	while
-다고 하다	to tell someone that S + V, people say + S + V
-도	too, also
-들	plural suffix
-라고 하다	to be called
-마다	every
-만	only
-밖에	just, only
-법	method; rule
-보다	than + N
-부터	from
-아/어/여 보다	to try + V-ing
-아/어/여 주다	to do something for someone

-아/어/여도	even if, even though
-아/어/여야 되다	have to, should, must
-의	of
-이랑	and
-지 마세요	Do not + V. (polite)
-지 않다	to not + A/V
-처럼	like, as if
-하고	and
-한테	to (someone)
1시간	one hour
4년	four years
가게	shop, store
가격	price
가깝다	to be close
가끔	sometimes
가능하다	to be possible
가다	to go
가로등	street lights
가르치다	to teach
가을	fall (season)
가장	the most
가전제품	home appliances
가져오다	to bring
가족	family
가지	eggplant
가짜	fake
가창력	singing ability
가치	value, worth
간	liver
갇히다	to be locked up
갈등	conflict
갈비	galbi (ribs)
갈아타다	to switch
감	persimmon
감기	cold, flu
감기(에) 걸리다	to catch a cold

감다	to wash (one's hair)
감동	being touched, being moved
감사합니다	Thank you.
값	price
갔다 오다	to go (somewhere) and come back
강남	Gangnam
강아지	puppy
강원도	Gangwon-do
강의	lecture
강의실	lecture room, classroom
같다	to be the same
같이	together with; like (something)
개	counter for things
개구리	frog
개다	to fold up
개미	ant
거	thing * This is a casual and colloquial word for 것.
거기	there, that place
거리	street, road, avenue
거의	almost
거짓말	lie
걱정	worry, concern
걱정되다	to be worried
건강	health
건조기	drying machine
걷다(1)	to walk
걷다(2)	to put away
걷히다	to be put away; to be cleared away
검	sword
검은깨	black sesame
검은깨 콩국수	black sesame soy noodles
검은색	black
검지	index finger
겁나다	to be scared

것	thing
겉	surface; outside
겉옷	outer clothing, outerwear
겨우	barely
겨울	winter
겨울날	winter days
결과	result
결석	absence
결심	resolution; determination
결심하다	to make up one's mind
결정	decision
결제	payment; settlement
결제하다	to pay
결혼하다	to marry
경쟁력	competitiveness
경쟁률	competition rate
경찰서	police station
경험	experience
계란	eggs
계속	repeatedly, again and again, continuously
고구마	sweet potato
고기	meat
고리	ring; hook
고민	worry, concern
고양이	cat
고장 나다	to be broken
곡	(a piece of) music
곧	soon
곳	place
공	ball
공기	air
공부하다	to study
과	department
과일	fruit
과일나무	fruit tree
관심	interest; attention

광화문	Gwanghwamun
괜찮다	to be okay
구	nine (sino-Korean number)
구름	clouds
구만	ninety thousand
구분	separation; classification
구십	ninety
국가 대표	national team
국내선	domestic flight
국립	national
국립대	national university
국물	soup, broth
국민	nation; people
군대	military
굳이	obstinately
굳히다	to harden, to solidify
굴	oysters
굵다	to be thick
권	counter for books
귀엽다	to be cute
귀찮다	to be too much work, to be a hassle
그	that, the
그거	that one, the thing, it, that * The original form of 그거 is 그것, but people often just use 그거 for ease of pronunciation.
그건	it * This word is shorthand for 그것은.
그것	that thing
그냥	just
그래서	so, therefore
그래요	exclamatory word used when reacting to someone with surprise or agreement
그래프	graph
그러게요	right, I know, yeah
그러면	if so, then
그런데	by the way

그럼	if so, then * This word is shorthand for 그러면.	길	road, street
그렇게	like that	길다	to be long
그렇다	to be like that	김	dried seaweed
그렇지만	but, however	김밥	gimbap (seaweed rice rolls)
그려지다	to be drawn	김치찌개	kimchi jjigae (kimchi stew)
그릇	bowl, dish	까다	to peel
그리다	to draw	깍두기	kkakdugi (diced radish kimchi)
그림	picture, painting, drawing	깨끗하다	to be clean
그립다	to miss (someone/something)	깨다	to break
그만	stop	깻잎	perilla leaf
그만두다	to quit	꼬리	tail
그분	the person (honorific)	꼭	for sure, absolutely
근데	by the way; but	꼭대기	top
근처	vicinity	꽂히다	to be hooked on (something)
글	writing; text	꽃	flower
글쎄	well (interjection)	꽃병	vase
긁다	to scratch	꽃잎	petal
금	gold	꽃향기	the scent of a flower
금방	a short time ago; immediately; quickly	꿀	honey
금요일	Friday	꿈	dream
금지	prohibition, ban	끄다	to turn off
급하다	to be urgent, to be hasty * 급하게 is the adverb form of 급하다.	끊임없이	constantly, ceaselessly
		끓다	to boil
		끝	end, finish
기	energy	끝나다	to be over
기다리다	to wait	끼	counter for meals
기대되다	to look forward to	(반지를) 끼다	to wear (a ring)
기본	basics; foundation	나	I
기본법	fundamental law	나가다	to go out
기사님	driver	나누기	division (÷)
기억	memory	나라	country
기억나다	to remember	나뭇잎	leaf
기자	reporter	나비	butterfly
기침약	cough medicine	나오다	to come out; to appear
기타	guitar; and so on	나이프	knife

How To Sound Like A Native Korean Speaker

난	as for me * This word is shorthand for 나는.	놀다	to hang out
난로	heater; stove	놀라다	to be surprised
날	day, date	놀이터	playground
날씨	weather	농구	basketball
날짜	date	농담	joke
남녀노소	men and women of all ages	높다	to be high; to be tall
남다	to be left, to remain	놓고 오다	to leave something behind
남대문	Namdaemun, the South Gate	놓다	to let go
남대문 시장	Namdaemun market	누가	who
낮	day, daytime	누구	who
낮잠	nap	누구나	everyone
내	my * 내 is short for 나의.	누구세요	Who are you?
내기	bet	누나	older sister (used by males)
내리다	to get off	눈	eye
내일	tomorrow	눈물	tear
냉동실	freezer compartment	눈병	eye infection
냉장실	fridge	눈알	eyeball
너	you	뉴스	news
너무	too (much), excessively	느낌	feeling; sense
넌	as for you * This word is the shorthand for 너는.	늘다	to increase, to improve
		늙다	to get old
널다	to hang	능력	ability, capability
넓다	to be spacious	늦여름	late summer
넘다	to be over (time/amount)	늦잠	oversleeping, late rising
넣다	to put in	닉네임	nickname
네(1)	yes; What?	다	all
네(2)	you, your	다녀오다	to go to a place and come back
네덜란드	Netherlands	다른	different; other
노래	song	다리미	iron
노래방	noraebang	다시	again
노래하다	to sing	다양하다	to be various, to be different
노량진	Noryangjin	다운로드	download
노트	notebook	다운로드 받다	to download (something)
논	rice paddy	다음	next, the following
		다음 주	next week
		다치다	to get hurt/injured

닦다	to wipe; to brush		도시	city
단단하다	to be firm		도와주다	to help
단어	word		도착하다	to arrive
닫다	to close, to shut		도토리	acorn
닫히다	to be closed		독립	independence
달	moon; month		독립하다	to move out (away from one's family)
달다	to be sweet		돈	money
달력	calendar		동	copper; east
닭갈비	dakgalbi (spicy stir-fried chicken with vegetables)		동네	neighborhood
닭고기	chicken meat		동대문	Dongdaemun
닮다	to resemble		동료	coworker, colleague
담	wall		동생	younger sibling
답	answer		동안	while, for, during
답답하다	to be frustrating/frustrated		동전	coin
답장	reply		돼지	pig
당	sugar; blood sugar; (political) party		돼지갈비	pork rib
당뇨	diabetes		되다(1)	to become, to reach a certain time or state
당연하다	to be natural; to be reasonable; to be fair		되다(2)	to be possible, to work
대기	waiting, stand-by		된장	doenjang (soybean paste)
대단하다	to be amazing, to be awesome		된장찌개	doenjang jjigae (soybean paste stew)
대답	answer, reply		두드리다	to knock; to beat
대부분	most of		두바이	Dubai
대통령	president		두부	tofu
대학	college		두유	soy milk
대학교	university, college		두통	headache
더	more		두통약	headache pill/tablet
더럽다	to be dirty		둘	two (native Korean number)
덕	virtue		뒤	back; after + N
덜다	to take some		뒤뚱뒤뚱 걷다	to waddle
덥다	to be hot		드디어	at last, finally
덧니	snaggletooth		드라마	drama
데	place * This is always used after a modifying word or phrase.		듣기	listening
			듣다	to listen
데이터	data		들	field
도	degree		들르다	to stop by

How To Sound Like A Native Korean Speaker

들리다	to be heard; to sound
들키다	to get caught
등	back
등록금	tuition
따뜻하다	to be warm
따로	separately
딱딱하다	to be hard
딸	daughter
땀	sweat
땀이 나다	to sweat
땅	land, ground
때	the time, the moment
때문	because of
떠들다	to talk loudly
떡	rice cake
떡볶이	tteokbokki (spicy rice cakes)
떨다	to shiver
떨어지다	to fall down
또	again, once more
똥	poop
뜀틀	vaulting box
뜰	yard
뜻	meaning
띄어쓰기	word spacing
라디오	radio
라면	ramen
랩	rap
러그	rug
러시아	Russia
레몬	lemon
레시피	recipe
로그인	login
로봇	robot
루머	rumor
리본	ribbon
리소토	risotto

리플레이	replay
마늘	garlic
마모	abrasion
마사지	massage
마스크	mask
마시다	to drink
마트	mart
막히다	to be stopped; to be blocked; to be clogged
만나다	to meet
만두	dumpling
만들다	to make
만족하다	to be satisfied
많다	to be a lot
많이	a lot * This is the adverb form of 많다.
말	words
말하기	speaking
맑다	to be clear
맘	mind; heart; feeling
맘껏	as much as one likes * This word is shorthand for 마음껏.
맘마미아	mamma mia
맛	taste, flavor
맛없다	to be not tasty
맛있다	to be tasty
맞다	to be correct, to be right
맞춤	assembling
맞춤법	spelling rules
맞히다	to be correct, to give the correct answer
매	rod; every; hawk
매주	every week
맵다	to be spicy
머리	head; hair; brain
머리숱	amount of hair
먹다	to eat

먼저	earlier; first
먼지	dust
멀미	motion sickness, travel sickness
멋있다	to look cool
멋지다	to be nice
메모	memo
메시지	message
멤버	member
며칠	a few days; what date
명	counter for people
명동	Myeongdong
명사	noun
명함	business card
몇	how many/much; what number; which
모든	all, every
모르다	to not know
모임	gathering
모자	hat
목	neck; throat
목록	list
목마르다	to be thirsty
목요일	Thursday
목표	target, goal
몰래	secretly
몸	body
몸매	body shape
몸무게	weight
못	cannot
못 하다	not able to do
못하다	cannot do; to be poor at something
무	radish
무게	weight
무늬	pattern
무료	free, no charge
무릎	knee

무슨	what
문	door
문법	grammar
문병	a visit to a sick person
문의	inquiry
문자	letter; text message
문제	problem; question
묻히다	to be buried
물	water
물개	seal
물고기	fish
물론	of course
물만두	boiled dumpling
물병	water bottle
물약	liquid medicine
물어보다	to ask (someone)
뭐	what
뭘	what * 뭘 is short for 무엇을.
미	mi (the musical note)
미국	America, American
미닫이	sliding door
미닫이문	sliding door
미안하다	to be sorry
미용	beauty care, hairdressing
밀다	to push
밑	bottom
바구니	basket
바깥	outside
바닐라	vanilla
바닷가	beach
바람	wind
바로	immediately
바르다[1]	to spread on
바르다[2]	to be straight; to be upright
바보	fool

바비큐	barbecue
바쁘다	to be busy
바이러스	virus
바이올린	violin
박물관	museum
밖	outside
반	class
반납하다	to return, to hand in, to turn in
반대	opposition
반드시	certainly; at any cost
반말	informal/casual language
반말하다	to use casual language, to speak in casual language
반지	ring
반팔	short-sleeved shirt
받다	to get, to receive
발	foot
발리	Bali
발전	development, advancement
발표	announcement; presentation
발표하다	to present, to make a presentation
밝다	to be bright
밟다	to step on
밤	night
밥	meal; cooked rice
밥맛	appetite
방	room
방문	visit
배	belly, stomach; boat; pear
배고프다	to be hungry
배꼽	navel
배낭여행	backpacking
배부르다	to be full
배우	actor/actress
배우다	to learn
백	hundred

백만장자	millionaire
밴	van
밸런타인데이	Valentine's Day
버리다	to throw away
버스	bus
버전	version
번개	lightning
번째	counter for ordinal numbers
벌	counter for clothing
벌레	worm; bug
벌써	already
범죄	crime
법	law
벤치	bench
벤티	Venti (drink size)
변하다	to change
별	star
별로	not really; not particularly
별명	nickname
별표	asterisk
병(1)	bottle, counter for bottles
병(2)	disease
볕	sunlight
보다	to see, to watch, to look; to meet
보물	treasure
보쌈	bossam (boiled pork wrap)
보이다	to be seen, to be visible
보통	usually
보푸라기	fluff, lint
보풀	fluff
복	luck, fortune
복잡하다	to be complicated
복지	welfare
복지법	welfare law
볼일	something to do; business

부끄럽다	to be shy	빈티지	vintage
부드럽다	to be soft	빌리다	to borrow
부딪히다	to bump	빚	debt, loan
부럽다	to be jealous	빛나다	to shine
부르다	to sing; to call	(살이) 빠지다	to lose weight
부모님	parents	빨갛다	to be red * 빨갛게 is the adverb form of 빨갛다.
부부	married couple		
부분	part	빨다	to wash (laundry)
부산	Busan	빨래	laundry
부엌	kitchen	빨리	quickly, fast
북마크	bookmark	빵	bread
분(1)	minute	빵값	price of bread
분(2)	honorific counter for people	빵집	bakery
분명히	clearly	뼈	bone
불	fire; light	뿌리	root
불가능하다	to be impossible	뿔	horn
불고기	bulgogi (marinated thin-sliced grilled meat)	삐	beep
		사 오다	to buy something and bring it
불만	dissatisfaction	사건	incident
불편하다	to be inconvenient	사고	accident
붐비다	to be crowded	사고 나다	an accident occurs
붙이다	to stick on	사다	to buy
비	rain	사다 주다	to buy something for someone and give it to them
비교	comparison		
비누	soap	사람	person, people, counter for people
비밀	secret		
비밀번호	password	사람들	people * -들 is a plural suffix.
비비다	to rub; to mix		
비빔밥	bibimbap (mixed rice with meat and assorted vegetables)	사랑하다	to love
		사립대	private university
		사용	use
비슷하다	to be similar	사용법	directions, instructions
비싸다	to be expensive	사정	reason, circumstances
비용	cost, expense	사탕	candy
비자	visa	산	mountain
비타민	vitamin	산꼭대기	the top of a mountain
비행기	plane	살(1)	flesh, fat
빅뉴스	big news	살(2)	counter for age

살다	to live		석류	pomegranate
살살 하다	to be gentle		선	line
삶	life		선물	gift
삶다	to boil		선물하다	to give something as a gift
삼	three; ginseng		선택하다	to make a choice
삼겹살	samgyeopsal (three layer pork belly)		설	Lunar New Year's Day
삼십	thirty		설날	Lunar New Year's Day * 날 means "day".
삼십육	thirty-six (sino-Korean number)		설마	No way; I doubt that.
상	prize, reward		설명하다	to explain
상상력	imagination		설치하다	to install
상의	discussion		섬	island
상추	lettuce		성격	personality, character
상추쌈	lettuce wrap		성공	success
새	new * 새 is always followed by a noun.		세금	tax
새싹	sprout		세다	to be strong * 세게 is the adverb form of 세다.
색연필	colored pencil		세련되다	to be sophisticated
샌드위치	sandwich		세제	detergent
샐러드	salad		셔틀버스	shuttle bus
생각	thought, memory		소	bull, cow
생각나다	to remember		소방서	fire station
생강	ginger		소시지	sausage
생기다⁽¹⁾	to look like		소식	news
생기다⁽²⁾	to arise		속	the inside
생일	birthday		손	hand
생일날	birthday		솔	brush
샤워	shower		솜씨	skill
샴푸	shampoo		쇼핑하다	to do one's shopping, to shop
서다	to stand, to stop walking		수건	towel
서두르다	to rush		수리	repair
서로	each other		수수료	commission; fee, charge
서른	thirty		수영	swimming
서른여섯	thirty-six (native Korean number)		수영하다	to swim
서울	Seoul		수용하다	to accommodate; to accept
서울역	Seoul Station		수원	Suwon

수원 화성	Suwon Hwaseong Fortress	시험	exam
수프	soup	식당	restaurant
순대	sundae (blood sausage)	식사	meal
순두부찌개	sundubu jjigae (spicy soft tofu stew)	신고	report; declaration
숨다	to hide	신기하다	to be surprising, to be amazing; to be surprised, to be amazed
숱	amount (of hair)	신다	to put on, to wear (shoes/socks)
숲	forest		
쉬	pee, wee-wee, tinkle	신랑	groom
쉬는 시간	break time	신발	shoes
쉬다	to have a break, to rest	신사	gentleman
쉰	fifty (native Korean number)	신청하다	to apply for
쉽다	to be easy * 쉽게 is the adverb form of 쉽다.	신촌	Sinchon
		신혼여행	honeymoon
쉿	shush	실	thread
슈렉	Shrek	실내	indoor
슈크림빵	cream puff	실수	mistake
스머프	Smurf	실수하다	to make a mistake
스물	twenty * Its modifying form is 스무.	실업률	unemployment rate
		싫다	to hate
스물넷	twenty-four (native Korean number) * Its modifying form is 스물네.	싫어하다	to dislike, to hate (transitive)
		심리학	psychology
		심리학과	department of psychology
스시	sushi	심장	heart
스케이트	skate	십만	hundred thousand
스태프	staff	십육	sixteen (sino-Korean number)
스테이크	steak	싱겁다	to be bland
스펀지	sponge	싸다⁽¹⁾	to be cheap
습관	habit	싸다⁽²⁾	to wrap
승무원	flight attendant	쌀	rice
시⁽¹⁾	poem	쌀쌀하다	to be chilly
시⁽²⁾	o'clock	쌈	lettuce wrap
시간	time; hours; session	쌍	pair
시다	to be sour	쌍시옷	the name of the consonant "ㅆ"
시작하다	to start, to begin	쏙	mimetic word describing the movement of entering something quickly
시장	market		
시청률	television ratings		
시키다	to order	쓰다⁽¹⁾	to be bitter

How To Sound Like A Native Korean Speaker

쓰다⁽²⁾	to write; to use	어디	where
쓰레기	trash	어때요	What do you think about...?, How about...?
씨	seed		to do (something) in a certain way
씨	honorific to refer to or call someone in a polite way	어떡하다	* This word is often used in the form of "어떡해(요)?" to mean, "What should we do?"
씻다	to wash		
아니다	to not be		how
아니요	No.	어떻게	* This is the adverb form of 어떻다.
아메리카노	Americano		
아무도	no one, nobody * 아무도 is always used in negative expressions.	어렵다	to be difficult
		어머	oh (interjection)
		어울리다	to suit
아무튼	anyway	어이없다	to be dumbfounded, to be at a loss for words
아버지	father		
아이	child, kid	어제	yesterday
아이들	children	어젯밤	last night
아이스크림	ice cream	어지럽다	to be dizzy
아직	still, yet	어학연수	language study abroad
아침	morning; breakfast	언제	when
아침밥	breakfast	얼굴	face
아파트	apartment	얼마	a small amount
아프다	to be sick, to hurt	얼마나	how + A/AD
안⁽¹⁾	in, inside	얼음	ice
안⁽²⁾	not	엄마	mother
안다	to hug	없다	to be not there, to not exist, to not have
앉다	to sit		
알다	to know	여가	leisure, spare time, free time
알람	alarm	여기	here
알아보다	to find out	여기요	Here you go.
알약	tablet, pill	여닫이	hinged door
앙코르	encore	여닫이문	swinging door
앞	front	여덟	eight (native Korean number)
액세서리	accessory	여의도	Yeouido
약속	promise; plan	여정	journey; itinerary
얘기하다	to talk * The original form of 얘기하다 is 이야기하다.	여행	trip
		역	station
		연기	acting; delay; smoke
어느	which	연락	contact

연습	practice
열	ten (native Korean number)
열쇠	key; clue
열심히	hard, diligently (adverb)
열여섯	sixteen (native Korean number)
열정	passion
열정적으로	passionately
영	zero
영어	English
영향력	influence
영화	movie
영화관	movie theater
옆	side
예쁘다	to be pretty
예약하다	to make a reservation
예의	manners, etiquette
예의 없이	rudely
옛날	the old days, the old times, the past
오늘	today
오다	to come
오렌지	orange (fruit)
오르다	to rise
오이	cucumber
오전	morning, a.m.
오징어	squid
온라인	online
올리브	olive
올해	this year
옷	clothes
와플	waffle
왜	why
왼쪽	the left side
요가	yoga
요가원	yoga studio
요거트	yogurt

요리	cooking
요일	day of the week
요정	fairy, elf
요즘	these days, recently
욕	swear word, curse
용	dragon
용어	term
우리	we, our
우와	wow (interjection)
우유	milk
운	luck
운동	exercise
운이 좋다	to be lucky
울리다	to ring
울산	Ulsan
원	the monetary unit of Korea
원룸	studio apartment (lit. one room)
월	month
월급날	payday
윗옷	top (clothing)
유행	trend
은	silver
은행	bank
을지로	Euljiro
음	umm (interjection)
음료수	drink, beverage
음식	food
음악	music
의미	meaning
의사	doctor
의사 선생님	doctor (honorific)
의사소통	communication
의자	chair
이(1)	this * This word is the adjective form of 이거.

이(2)	teeth
이거	this one
이렇게	like this, this way
이모티콘	emoticon
이미지	image
이번	this time
이사 오다	to move in
이야기	story
이야기하다	to tell
이제	now, now that
인기	popularity
인기가 많다	to be popular
인분	serving
인생	life
인천	Incheon
일(1)	one (sino-Korean number)
일(2)	day
일(3)	work, job
년	year
일단	first, for now, once
일자리	job, work
일정	program; schedule, itinerary
읽다	to read
잃어버리다	to lose
입	mouth
입다	to wear
입력	input, entry
입맛	appetite
입장	admission, entrance
입장권	entrance ticket
입장료	admission, entrance fee
있다	to be there, to have, to exist
있잖아요	You know what?
자	ruler
자격	qualification
자다	to sleep

자동	automatic
자동차	car
자랑	boast
자료	material
자르다	to cut
자리	place, space, seat
자매	sisters
자물쇠	lock
자장	a magnetic field
자전거	bicycle
자주	often
작년	last year
작다	to be small
잔	counter for glasses or cups
잔소리	nagging
잘	well (adverb)
잘리다	to get fired
잘못하다	to do (something) wrong
잘하다	to be good at (something)
잠	sleep
잠그다	to lock up
잠들다	to fall asleep
잠자리	dragonfly * It is pronounced [잠자리].
잠자리	bed * It is pronounced [잠짜리].
잡히다	to get caught
장	counter for paper
장르	genre
장마	rainy season
재미없다	to be boring
재미있다	to be fun/interesting
저(1)	I, me (honorific)
저(2)	that
저금	saving, savings
저기	there, over there
저기요	Excuse me.

저녁	evening; dinner
저녁밥	dinner
저번	the other day
저희	we, our (honorific)
적응력	adaptability
전	jeon (savory Korean pancake)
전	before, ago
전공	major (in school)
전기	electricity
전등	light, light bulb
절대	absolutely; never
젊다	to be young
점	dot, point
점수	score
점심	lunch
점심밥	lunch
점점	gradually
정도	degree
정류장	stop, station
정말	really; fact
정확하다	to be precise * 정확하게 is the adverb form of 정확하다.
제	I (polite) (subject), my (honorific) * 제 is short for 저의.
제발	please
제일	first; most
제주도	Jeju Island
젤리	gummy candy
조각	piece
조건	condition
조금	a little
조명	lights
조사	to be investigating, investigation
조심하다	to be careful
조언	advice

조용하다	to be quiet
조용히	quietly * This word is the adverb form of 조용하다.
족발	jokbal (seasoned and steamed pig feet)
졸다	to boil down
좀(1)	a little bit * This is shorthand for 조금.
좀(2)	please
종류	kind, sort, category, type
종이	paper
종이컵	paper cup
좋다	to like, to be good
좋아하다	to like (transitive)
죄	sin
죄송합니다	I am sorry.
주	week
주다	to give
주로	usually
주말	weekend
주머니	pocket
주문하다	to order
주변	surroundings, around
주소	address
주스	juice
주의	caution, attention, warning
주장	argument, claim
주제	subject, topic
주차장	parking lot
죽	porridge
줄넘기	jump rope
줍다	to pick up
중(1)	among
중(2)	in, in the middle of
중요하다	to be important
지그재그	zigzag
지금	now

How To Sound Like A Native Korean Speaker

지난주	last week	처음	first
지루하다	to be boring	천	thousand
지치다	to get tired	첫인상	first impression
지하	basement	청소	cleaning
지하철	subway	초콜릿	chocolate
진주(1)	pearl	최고	best
진주(2)	Jinju (a city in Korea)	최고 기온	peak temperature
진짜	really, truly, so, very	최신	newest
진하다	to be thick	최악	the worst
짐	burden, load	추다	to dance
집	house; store	추로스	churros
집값	house price	추천	recommendation
집중	concentration	춘천	Chuncheon
짜다	to be salty	출구	exit
짜장	black bean sauce	출동	move out, mobilize
짜장면	jjajangmyeon (black bean noodles)	출발	departure, leave
짜증 나다	to be irritated, to be annoyed	출발하다	to depart
짧다	to be short * 짧게 is the adverb form of 짧다.	출생률	birth rate
		춤	dance
		춥다	to be cold
쪽	page	취업률	employment rate
찌개	stew	층	floor
찜	steamed dish	치다(1)	to draw, to mark
찜닭	jjimdak (braised chicken with vegetables)	치다(2)	to play (an instrument)
찜질방	public bathhouse, sauna	치마	skirt
차(1)	car	치즈	cheese
차(2)	tea	친구	friend
차갑다	to be cold	칠	seven (sino-Korean number)
차다	to kick	침	saliva; acupuncture
차장	deputy chief	카드	card
착륙	landing	카페 라테	caffe latte
참	very	칸	room, space
참고하다	to refer to	칼	knife
참다	to hold back	칼날	the blade of a knife
찾다	to look for; to find	캐다	to dig up
책	book	커피	coffee

커피값	price of coffee	트림	burp, belching
커피숍	coffee shop	특히	especially, particularly
케이크	cake	틀	cast, outline, frame
코감기	sinus cold	틀다	to turn on
코끝	the tip of one's nose	틀리다	to be wrong
코끼리	elephant	틈	crack, gap
코피	nosebleed	티셔츠	T-shirt
콜라	Coke	티켓	ticket
콜라병	Coke bottle	파일	file
콧노래	humming	판	counter for a whole pizza, cake, etc.
콧물	runny nose	팔	arm; eight
콩	bean	팔다	to sell
콩국수	cold soybean noodle soup	팔찌	bracelet
크다	to be big	팥빵	red bean bread
큰아들	one's eldest son	패션	fashion
키	height	팩	facial mask
타다(1)	to ride, to take (vehicle)	팬	fan
타다(2)	to be burned	팬티	underpants
탄산음료	soda, carbonated drink	퍼센트	percent
탈(1)	mask; trouble	펀치	punch
탈(2)	illness, sickness	페이지	page
탈의실	fitting room, locker room	펴다	to spread out
탈이 나다	to get sick	편리하다	to be convenient
탑	tower	편의점	convenience store
탕	soup	편하다	to be comfortable
태도	attitude	평균	average
택배	parcel delivery service	평범하다	to be plain, to be common, to be typical
턱	chin	평창	Pyeongchang
털	hair, fur	포장	packaging; gift-wrapping
털다	to dust	포장하다	to wrap
털리다	to be robbed	포크	fork
통	bucket, container	폰	phone * It is short for 휴대폰 or 핸드폰, which means "mobile phone".
퇴근하다	to leave work, to get off work		
투덜이	grouchy	표	ticket; table (chart)
튀김	fried food	표현	expression, representation
튜브	tube		

풀	grass; glue; pool	호선	subway line
프랑스	France	호텔	hotel
프랑스어	French	혹시	by any chance
플래시	flashlight	홍대	Hongdae
피	blood	화이트	white
피부	skin	화장실	restroom
피부병	skin disease	화장품	cosmetics
피아노	piano	확률	probability, chance
피자	pizza	활동	activity, movement, campaign
피자집	pizza place	활동하다	to work
핀란드	Finland	회사	company
하나	one (native Korean number) * Its modifying form is 한.	회의	meeting, conference
하다	to do	훑어보다	to glance over, to skim
하루	one day	훨씬	much (more)
학교	school	휠체어	wheelchair
학생	student	흘리다	to spill
한국	Korea	희다	to be white
한국말	Korean language	희망	hope, wish
한국어	Korean language	희생	sacrifice
한라산	Mt. Halla	흰색	white color
한여름	midsummer	흰자	the white part of an egg or eyeball
한집	the same house	힌트	hint
한참	a long time	힘들다	to be hard, to be difficult
합격률	acceptance rate		
합정	Hapjeong		
핫도그	hot dog		
항공	flight		
항공권	plane ticket		
해돋이	sunrise		
햄버거	burger		
햇볕	sunshine		
행동하다	to act, to behave		
험하다	to be rough		
협력	cooperation, collaboration		
형용사	adjective		

Learn More Effectively with Our Premium Courses

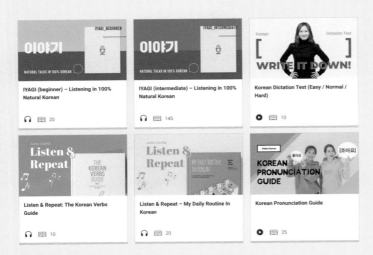

IYAGI (beginner) – Listening in 100% Natural Korean

🎧 📖 20

IYAGI (intermediate) – Listening in 100% Natural Korean

🎧 📖 145

Korean Dictation Test (Easy / Normal / Hard)

▶ 📖 10

Listen & Repeat: The Korean Verbs Guide

🎧 📖 10

Listen & Repeat – My Daily Routine In Korean

🎧 📖 20

Korean Pronunciation Guide

▶ 📖 25

Gain unlimited access to hundreds of video and audio lessons by becoming a Premium Member at our website, **https://talktomeinkorean.com!** Practice your pronunciation and further improve your listening skills through our online courses.

Courses available online include our Korean Pronunciation Guide course, which is directly related to this book, Korean Dictation Test course, Listen & Repeat course, and more.

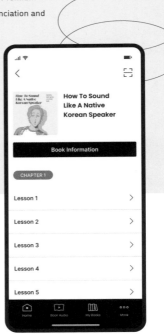

TTMIK Book Audio App

Download our app **TTMIK: Audio** to listen to all the audio and video tracks from our book conveniently on your phone! The app is available for free on both iOS and Android. Search for **TTMIK: Audio** in your app store.